BORN FOR ARCHAEOLOGY

BORN FOR ARCHAEOLOGY
An Autobiography

H.D. SANKALIA

© H.D. Sankalia

B·R·Publishing Corporation

Published by :   B.R. Publishing Corporation
                     461, Vivekanand Nagar Delhi-110052
Distributed by :   D.K. Publishers' Distributors,
                     1, Ansari Road, Darya Ganj
                     NEW DELHI-110052   Phone : 274819
Printed by :   S.K. TRADERS
                     2/34, Roop Nagar
                     DELHI-110007

CONTENTS

CONTENTS

One

Birth, Childhood and Education

1. *Not trained but born to be an archaeologist*
2. *Childhood* 3. *Captain of a Cricket Team*
4. *Long Walks* 5. *Epic Stories* 6. *The Aryans*
7. *Writer* 8. *History Scholarship* 9. *First Research Paper* 10. *Nālandā, LL.B. and M.A.*
11. *Marriage* 12. *Harijan Movement and Swadeshi* 13. *Father Heras.*

IN my undergraduate class I was a student of Sanskrit and English, while for the M.A. degree I wrote a thesis on the University of Nālandā for which I had to study history or, to be more precise, Ancient Indian History. Thus, I never studied archaeology during my college days. And though I got a Ph. D. degree in archaeology, I was never a student of this discipline whether in India or abroad. Ancient Indian History first introduced me to inscriptions, and then to architecture and afterwards to sculpture, iconography, numismatics, and epigraphy and finally to archaeology.

Still more wonderful—and I believe it is providential—was my introduction to prehistory, which later became my life-work. That is what Rao Bahadur Dikshit, a former Director-General of Archaeology of India, remarked one day standing under the doorway of my room in the Jejeebhoy Castle in Pune. Archaeology brought me in touch with geology,

2   palaeontology, climatology, and ethnography. Thus, in one way or the other, all major aspects of archaeology I have had occasion to handle. Some of my friends have called me a versatile genius and though I feel greatly flattered by this description, people have wondered how all this became possible. The only answer that I can give now is that I found it actually recorded in a book on astrology, called *Bhrigu Saṁhitā*, that a person born under such-and-such planetary conjunction (*yoga*) will one day be an archaeologist. And I happen to have been born under such a conjuction. Two other similar *saṁhitas* confirmed this prediction, though their descriptions were not as precise as the one in *Bhrigu Saṁhitā*. They also said that the person born under such-and-such planetary conjunction would be interested in *all old things*. Thus, behind all my actions one can see the hand of an invisible driving force. I think this is more or less true of all human beings, but in many persons it is not as evidently clear as in my case.

Another trait of my character was explained a few months ago, after I had prepared the first draft of this autobiography.

Two young followers of Krishna Consciousness Movement, one a young man of about twenty, an Englishman and the other, an American, happened to come to our residence to tell us about this Movement. Both the young followers were well-read, and knew Sanskrit also. I found them to be very sincere devotees of Shri Krishna. The elder one happened to be an amateur astrologer as well. Somehow he got interested in us and requested us to show him our horoscopes. On seeing my horoscope, he told me that though I must have made some money, I would renounce everything. I asked him what made him say so. He explained to me that it was because Jupiter in the 9th House in my horoscope indicated that I would choose the vocation of a real *guru*. Not only has such a person the desire

and ability to teach, but a tendency to renounce
all that he has gathered in his life through his profession.

This reading was remarkably true of my life, and
in consonance with my ways of thinking. Not only
have I guided a large number of students, particularly at the Ph. D. level, but even now I would like
to meet young students and help them understand
this or that subject. As far back as 1958, I had
thought of building a small house on the campus of
the Deccan College, if the Trustees permitted me to
build one by granting a piece of land with a definite
legal contract that the house, after the death of
both of us—myself and my wife—would belong to
the College. This suggestion the Trustees had readily
accepted.

Moreover, all the books that I have—and there
are quite a few and many of them quite expensive—
I have presented to the College Library. Further,
I have also made a provision in my will for the
physical expansion of the department, as the present
one is indeed insufficient. God willing, this last wish
will also be fulfilled.

Not only this, but I have a strong desire to
donate my body. As soon as I die let the limbs of my
body such as the cornea of the eyes, and the kidneys
(if they are in good condition), be immediately
removed, and used for transplantation or stored for
future use. The rest of the body may be skinned,
and the skin also used for grafting. The articulated
skeleton might then be presented to a medical college
or the Department of Archaeology, if they so desire.
Thus both the mortal remains and other effects will
be utilised for the benefit of the students.

2

As my mother's health was indifferent I was
born so subnormal in weight and size that the doctor

4　who had attended to my birth gave up all hopes of my survival. Thin and rickety, I looked no bigger than a mouse, so my mother told me. However, I survived and though I never picked up much flesh and fat, I was very lively. I could never sit still or quiet, with the result that while hardly two years old, I scalded my hand with a pot of boiling water. But for the doctor's prompt treatment I would have died certainly. The accident, however, left a deep scar on my left hand. I do not know why I always like to play with boiling water; and may be because of this there are very few days in my life when I have not heated up water for making tea. Vivaciousness is my second nature. I must have some physical work to do—be it walking, running or gardening. In my childhood I spent more than half the day flying kites, playing cricket or *gillīdaṇḍā*. During the monsoon when we could not play outdoor games, we played cards but I always liked outdoor games.

3

When I grew up I formed my own cricket team and played this game right up to my M. A. class and liked it so much and played it so well that the members of the staff and students at the Deccan College were surprised to see me on the occasion of the college annual day that I could bowl, bat, and field as well as a seasoned player even at the age of sixty.

Captainship of the cricket team (which comprised most of the residents of the building where we lived in C.P. Tank, Bombay) not only gave me a bit of opportunity of organizing and running a concern on no-loss-no-profit basis, but it also taught me how and when to take a firm action. Thus, if the situation demanded I did not hesitate to expel a player from the field ; of course, such occasions came but once or twice during the course of ten years. The love of outdoor games gave me stamina enough though I remained always lean and thin.

To the love of cricket was added the love of long walks, particularly in the countryside; a love which came to be developed gradually. Almost twice a year, my parents used to go to Matheran or Lonavala or Deolali. Usually we stayed in a " sanatorium" (a guest-house is called sanatorium in such places). Here I would go out with my father almost everyday to the distant "points", and walking ten to fifteen miles a day was no problem for me. In spite of taking long walks everyday I appeared very weak. In 1929 I had accompanied my brother-in-law's eldest son, Kapil and his younger brother and sister to Mahabaleshwar. Kapil was then recuperating from typhoid. One day a guest came to meet us, and he was surprised when he was told that Kapil, and not I, was the invalid who had been recuperating ! Thus nobody would believe that I was capable of enduring such physical hardships. I did not know then my habit of long walks would pay me dividends one day when as an archaeologist I would trudge long distances in plains, dales, and hills.

5

From a very early age I also developed an intense love for the stories of our epics—the *Rāmāyaṇa* and the *Mahābhārata*—and the *Puranas* particularly the *Bhāgavata*. By the age of ten I had already read these stories in Gujarati translations as well as the lives of Napolean I, Shivaji, and Rana Pratap and the whole of Tod's *Rajasthan*. In fact, I would not sleep unless my father told me a story. Thus was created a desire to know our past, though I am sure I did not know then even the word "archaeology". These stories moulded my attitude to life. Of the many striking incidents, the one that impressed me most was Napoleon's march to Jena and Austerlitz and his brilliant victory when he was thwarted from his attempt to cross the English

Channel by Nelson. The lesson that I derived from this incident was : "If not this, then that ; but never sit still with folded hands".

6

The desire to know our past took a definite shape in May 1924. At that time I was staying with my parents in a 'sanatorium' at Nasik. I had appeared for the matriculation examination the second time because I had failed to pass the first time by four marks in General English. The 'sanatorium' had a library. In it I found a Gujarati translation of Bal Gangadhar Tilak's *The Arctic Home in the Vedas*. I read through this book though I do not know how much of it I then understood. But one thing that impressed me was that I should do something to know about the Aryans in India for which, I thought, a good knowledge of Sanskrit and Mathematics would be necessary. So at the age of fifteen or thereabout I decided to opt for Sankrit for the degree of B.A. I also decided to do mathematics in the first year of Intermediate Arts examination. This was the most important decision from which I did not deviate in the least. And knowing how indecisive Indian students are my decision must be regarded as something "providential".

7

The second year of matriculation examination was also a turning point in my career from another angle, for it laid the foundation of my career as a writer. The Elphinstone High School had then a new Principal whose name was Katti. Though he was a Senior Wrangler, he taught us General English. He soon found out that I was not such a bad student as to fail in General English, for in the weekly examination I had secured 29 marks out of 50. He called me one day in his office and advised me to get over my nervousness, for he thougt that nervousness was the main reason that I had failed.

He also wanted me to write out what I had read in
the morning instead of reading the same thing again
and trying to commit it to memory. I followed his
advice as best as I could and when I joined the
St. Xavier's College next year, I could prepare my
own notes after listening to the professors' lectures.
These notes were avidly sought by my fellow-stu-
dents. At St. Xavier's College I also wrote essays on
general topics which Father Fell and Father Dhur
would want us to write from time to time. On the
strength of one of these essays, my name was included on the list of students selected for some special
coaching.

8

I did well in the Intermediate Arts examination
getting a high second. And though I stood second in
"History and Administration" I decided to stick to
my original plan, made as far as 1924, namely to
take up Sanskrit, and not History, for my B.A.
examination. I would have been a student of History
in B.A. class had I been, according to first valuation,
placed first in "History and Administration". For,
then I would have been the recipient of Wordsworth
Scholarship which required the scholarship holder
to take up History and Politics in B.A. But my
answer-book was re-examined by a panel of exami-
ners, and since I had answered the last question
giving only the outline and not fully, it was decided
to grace the other student by two marks and place
him first. I learnt these details later from our
teacher, Professor Lala, a Sindhi. He did not
know that I belonged to St. Xavier's College.

In my undergraduate class I, therefore, took
Honours in Sanskrit and Voluntary English. The
latter also included the study of textual criticism.
Here we had to study *King Lear* and Bradley's Shakes-
perian criticism. Bradley aroused my latent facul-
ties of textual criticism. I do not know how I wrote
a fine essay on *King Lear*. Both my nephew, who was

then in the final year of B.A. class and my uncle were surprised to see that a boy who had failed in General English in the matriculation examination could write an original essay on *King Lear*.

But that was not all. We had to study four or five Sanskrit plays. One of them was *Kundamālā* by Dinnaga. The theme was so similar to that of Bhavabhuti's *Uttara-Rāmacharita*, which I had occasion to study in the Intermediate Arts class, that I thought that the theme of *Uttara-Rāmācharita* must have been based on *Kundamālā*. The idea gripped me so much that I got up from my bed one day at midnight and wrote out a very detailed comparison and substantiated each of my statements by giving illustrations from the texts.

9

At that time Father Zimmermann used to teach us Sanskrit. Like all German Indologists he too was known for his criticial insight. One day I casually spoke to Fr Zimmermann about my paper. He immediately called me to his room at the St. Xavier's College and asked me to read out the whole paper to him. He was so much impressed by this comparison that he asked me to read it before the Sanskrit Society. I read out this paper entitled *"Kundamala* and *Uttara-Ramacharita* and argued logically, step by step, how Bhavabhuti had improved upon Dinnaga's *Kundamālā*. Prof. K.M. Shembhavnekar, a Sanskrit scholar who was present got very excited, and remarked that a poet of Bhavabhuti's calibre could never have imitated an unknown poet like Dinnāga. In fact, he said, it should be the other way round. However, my arguments were cogent enough and the treatment was unimpeachable so much so that when I thought of re-publishing this article in 1966, after nearly thirty-seven years, not a word had to be changed and, what is more, my views, far from being challenged, were supported by a Bengali scholar who wrote a much larger work on Dinnāga's *Kuṇḍamālā*.   9

About 1929-30 I was also doing some research
under Father Heras in his newly founded Indian
Historical Research Institute in Bombay. It appears
that Fr Zimmermann had spoken to Fr Heras and
others about my article on *"Kuṇḍamala* and *Uttara-
Ramacharita"*. So Fr Heras called me to his room and
told me that he was quite sure that I would do very
well as a research student whether in history or in
Sanskrit. B.A. examination over, I gave up Sanskrit
and began to study Ancient Indian History under
Fr Heras. Naturally, this disappointed Fr Zimmermann. But I told him the kind of career I had
chalked out for myself when I was appearing in
matriculation examination and I think he was satisfied by my explanation.

10

At the Indian Historical Research Institute, I
gave up my research on Pulakeśi II, the famous
Chālukyan King of Bādāmi, and selected a totally
new subject—the University of Nālandā. A topic
like this is multidimensional. While from the history
of ancient Indian literature I could reconstruct the
history of Nālandā with comparative ease, thanks to
my knowledge of Sanskrit; totally new subjects such
as art, architecture, and iconography had to be
newly learnt to do justice to the subject. These subjects I did not study formally and I picked up these
disciplines directly by acquainting myself with the
objects of art and architecture and reading about
them. Of course, this was how my *guru* Fr Heras had
himself learnt these things. What he did in mycase
was to give me the opportunity to accompany him to
Nālandā and many other ancient sites in U. P. and
Bihar, ending with a trip to Calcutta and its splendid museum.

Up to that time, I had gone only to places near
Bombay, such as Nasik, Deolali and Lonavala, Mat-

heran and Mahabaleshwar and that too with my parents. I had also seen such ancient monuments as at Karla, Bhaja, and Kanheri.

The trip to Nālandā was undertaken towards the close of the second year of my M.A. Normally, many students completed their thesis within this period. I was also anxious to do so. But some difficult problems were cropping up. While reading about Nālandā and its contribution to ancient India and Buddhist iconography, I found many references to Tantrism (or Tantricism). What this *ism* was had to be first understood. So I was advised to go to Dr Benoytosh Bhattacharya at Baroda. Bhattacharya had published a fine book on Buddhist iconography. At Baroda he placed so much material at my disposal that instead of completing my thesis in 1931, I decided to do so a year later. During the interval I read not only all about Tantrism, but got through my second LL.B. examination, thus assuring my father and uncle that I was not wasting my time but was doing what both of them, particularly my uncle had expected me to do, namely to join our family business of practising at the courts. I submitted the thesis as I had planned. It should have fetched me not only a First Class, but the Chancellor's Medal as well (which at that time was awarded only to the students of History) as my *guru* had expected. But my referee, who was no less a scholar than the late Professor K.T. Shah, the economist turned culture-historian, pointed out that the section on Tantrism was unduly long and that, according to him, marred the overall excellence of the thesis. Of course, this I had done at the suggestion of Bhatta-charya. Anyway I was not at all disappointed. Nor were my father and uncle. Both of them were then anxious that I should settle down in life, join the family firm of lawyers and get married.

11

But I did not agree. There were several

reasons which I must mention here briefly just to tell my readers how a sensitive youth can be disturbed by the unimaginative people around him. First, since 1921, inspired by Gandhiji, we had all taken to wearing *Khadi*. I had actually made a bonfire of my "merchat cap", for it was thought that we must boycott foreign cloth. Secondly, I personally believed in having a very simple, unostentatious marriage function not only for myself but for all— the rich and the poor alike. So I scrupulously avoided attending such functions as the "caste dinners" and marriages. Thirdly, I abhorred my physical weakness and I thought I was not fit enough to marry. All these had made me to decide against early marriage. I was also afraid that my future wife might not share my views on simplicity in marriage rites and rituals. I had decided, therefore, not to marry, though because of the status of our family and my educational qualifications several good offers of marriage my parents received now and then from Surat and Bombay. There was also another important decision that I had made then and that was not to marry unless I had started earning my livelihood.

To these personal reasons political events gave an additional edge. Mahatma Gandhi had once again embarked upon a fast unto death. This time he undertook the fast for the sake of the Harijans and to prevent Dr Ambedkar from giving them a separate political and social status. Students were being advised to go on indefinite strike by the student leaders like Asoka Mehta. Asoka was junior to me and had attended my lectures on Ancient Indian History.

12

I was drawn into this movement because at that time I was giving tuition to the daughter of a staunch Congress worker in Bombay. The entire family was so Congress-oriented that meetings were

12 held at their house in Girgaum Back Road—now
Vithalbhai Patel Road. During one of these political discussions, I heard that Asoka Mehta was advising students to go on an indefinite strike. I told
one of his brothers: "What is needed is some practical work for the cause which is dear and near to
Gandhiji instead of strike". He conveyed this advice
to Asoka Mehta who invited me to address a gathering of students. This was my first—and last—encounter with politics. But the matter did not rest
there. I was asked to prepare a scheme for practical
work to be done among the Harijans by the late
Manu Subedar who held an important position in
the Congress. Accordingly, we visited a number of
Harijan *chawls*. I also accompanied groups of student workers who would campaign from house to
house, preaching *swadeshi* and the use of *khadi*. The
"Belapur Sugar" had just then appeared in the
market. We took samples of this sugar from house
to house to popularise it but compared to the sugar-
like *"moras"* from Mauritius, this was expensive
and not normally preferred by the housewives.

My father got scent of these activities and he
thought that I might be clapped in jail. So to wean
me away he decided to take me to Matheran. As
usual, I had to accompany him. Matheran this time
was destined to play a memorable part in my life
for it was here that I met my "future" wife. We
were neighbours in the sanatorium. Her mother
was widowed at a very young age of sixteen with
two children—a daughter of three years and a son
aged one-and-a-half years. Though highly connected, Taraben had decided to eke out an independent
life by giving tuitions in English and music. Because of this she and her children had developed an
independent attitude in life.

Sarla, the daughter of Taraben, shared my love
of outdoor games and also liked to go out for long
walks. Naturally this close association developed
into mutual love for each other. Though this was

noticed by my parents and Taraben, the matter
remained just at that level. In June my examination
results were declared. So Taraben came to our house
in C.P. Tank to congratulate me and invited me to
their house at Lamington Road.

Another development was also taking place at
that time. Since I had passed the second year of
LL.B., my father and uncle wanted me to join the
family firm of pleaders. My uncle, Nathukaka,
suggested, taking into consideration my shy nature
and week constitution, that I should sign the articles
and become a Solicitor. He had concluded that I
was fit for indoor life and desk-work only. But my
father took a slightly different view. He said that he
would leave the matter to me, though he, perhaps,
thought that my uncle's suggestion was not only
right but also practical.

13

Fr Heras, my *guru*, thought quite differently.
Knowing me much more intimately than my uncle
and my father, he felt that I should go to England
and get a Ph.D. in archaeology. This suggestion was
a surprise to me. For I had never dreamt of going
abroad. Nor were we affluent enough so as to
"waste" several thousands of rupees in a foreign
country. I was also not sure what job I would get
after I had returned from England. I shared all
these fears with Fr. Heras. He said in his characteristic way, "Hasmukh (my first name), I know all
that. What I can assure you is that you will do
well. You are fit to be an archaeologist, though I
cannot hold out any guarantee that a post will be
waiting for you when you return. Or that someone
would die and a post would fall vacant just for you!"

Fr Heras then accompanied me to the University
to consult various people regarding courses in the
Universities of Oxford and Cambridge. Finding
that a knowledge of Greek and Lati

14 quired of a Ph. D. student, I ruled out these famous seats of learning, though I liked to be a student in one of these universities. London at that time was unknown to most of us. However, Fr Heras knew K. de B. Codrington, who was then the Curator of the Indian Section of the Victoria and Albert Museum in South Kensington. He advised me to join the University College and not the School of Oriental Studies in London, because archaeology was not taught by the latter Institution. He further suggested that I should work on the "Dynastic Study of Monuments" for my Ph. D. So he advised the School of Oriental Studies to transfer my admission from there to the University of London.

At this time—September-October, 1933—an International Conference was being held at Warsaw in Poland, and it was decided that I should attend it with Fr Heras and then proceed to London. But fate had willed otherwise. Learning about all these developments, Taraben suggested that I should marry her daughter and then go abroad. To this suggestion I immediately replied that I had long ago made up my mind not to marry, and if at all I do, it will be only after I got settled in life.

This reply certainly came as a rude shock to Sarla and her mother. I stopped going to their house at Lamington Road. These events also caused much mental tension which ultimately upset my constitution, frail as it always was. I suffered from severe diarrhea which was diagnosed after two months as due to nervous disorder. What was needed was a change of surroundings and sympathetic treatment. So I went to my cousin, an uncle's daughter at Malabar Hills. Here, gradually I recovered, so much so that I could complete a prize essay which I had written under a pen-name on the "*Chaitya* Caves in the Bombay Presidency" for the Bhagwanlal Indraji Prize and Gold Medal. Hardly had I recovered from several months' attack of nervous diarrhea, when I had an attack of typhoid.

Fortunately, this did not last long nor did it leave
me completely debilitated, as this foul disease
usually does.

The wonder was that my long illness, the first of
the kind in my life, did not shake my parents' resolve to send me to England though they were some-
what ill at ease because of my weak constitution,
and particularly my inability to eat any kind of
food anywhere. I spent that summer vacation at
Mahabaleshwar with my would-be mother-in-law
and her children. Here I corrected the proofs of
the thesis on the Nālandā University which was
being printed at a press in Madras. The University
of Bombay had given a publication grant of Rs. 750
on the recommendation of P.V. Kane who had
liked it very much and wanted a few more illustrations to be included in it.

Though I could not avail of the unique opportunity to accompany Fr Heras to Poland, I got another opportunity and that was to teach Ancient
Indian History to the M.A. students in the absence
of Fr Heras. This was a purely private arrangement—possible only at that time when rules and
regulations were not as stringent as they are now.
Otherwise how could a fresh M.A., without any
previous teaching experience lecture to the M.A.
class? This was not an interlude, but a necessary
first step in the formation of my career. A thesis.
however well written, helps a student in knowing or mastering only a few aspects of a subject
well enough but many corners of his mind remain
unilluminated. These can be more fully lighted by
teaching alone. A teacher must acquire an overall knowledge of the subject that he teaches to
satisfy the varying needs of his students. And this
is exactly what had happend. I had to teach the
Gupta Period about which I had read a good deal
while doing my thesis on Nālandā. But for teaching
I had to wade through all the inscriptions of the
Guptas and those of their contemporaries, besides

16   the relevant books on the subject. More than
knowledge the experience was useful. At first,
I was a little nervous, for many of the students were
of my age or even older. However, I used to prepare well, and the lectures were well-attended
though I do not know whether it was because atten-
dance was compulsory.

Dr. H.D. Sankalia
Date of birth - 10 - 12 - 1908
Place of birth - Bombay
Time - Approx. Between
5 - To. 6 am

जन्म लग्न कुंडली

ग्रह	र	चं	मं	बु	गु	शु	श	रा	के	ह	ने	प्लू
राशि	७	३	६	७	४	६	११	२	८	८	३	२
अंश	२५	०	७	२०	२१	२३	१०	४	४	३३	२४	२
कला	३०	१०	३०	३०	२८	२०	५०	८	८	१४	४	२८

स्पष्ट ग्रह

चन्द्र - पुनर्वसु - ४ था चरण कर्क राशि

Horoscope of Prof. H. D. Sankalia

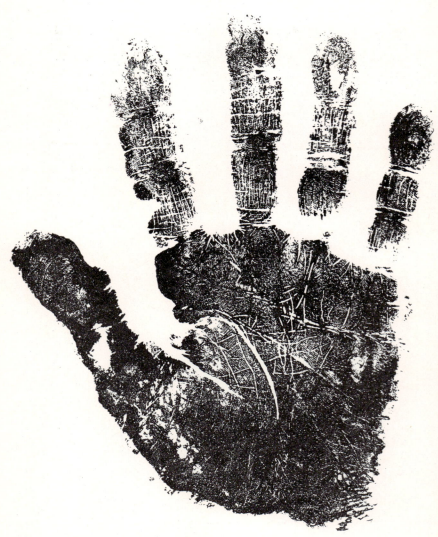

Right hand palm impression of Prof. H. D. Sankalia

Prof. H. D. Sankalia, 1974.

Smt. Moti Gauri Dhiraj Lal
Mother of Prof. H. D. Sankalia

Shri Dhiraj Lal V. Sankalia
Father of Prof. H. D. Sankalia

'Sachchidananda', the personal house of Prof. Sankalia in the Deccan College campus. In the foreground, Prof. Sankalia is seen sitting with his wife.

Sankalia with his wife, Smt. Sarala Devi, 1937.

The old building of the Deccan College, now housing the Library, etc.

Two young colleagues of Prof. Sankalia, Dr. R.K. Pant
and Shri Sardari Lal, near a gravel deposit at
Pahalgam, Kashmir; June, 1969. The team
made the rare discovery of Palaeoliths.

The new building of the Department of Archaeology,
Deccan College, Pune

In London

I left for England in September 1934. My parents, Sarla and many of my relatives had come to see me off at the Ballard Pier (Bombay) where I boarded the ship. Naturally, I felt the wrench of separation and I wept a great deal. Instead of voyaging all the way round, I got down at *Marseilles* and went by the overland route to Calais and then over to Dover. An elderly friend who used to live in our building had advised me as well as his nephew who had left earlier to travel by the *de luxe* train. This both of us did but found on reaching London that it was considered a great luxury indulged in only by the very rich. Normally ordinary people, and particularly students, travelled third.

In London I had no difficulty at all because I had many friends there and one friend who lived in the same building in C. P. Tank, as ourselves, in Bombay had already booked a small appartment for me at 34, Norfolk Square, near Hyde Park. This was considered a good locality and the rent was comparatively high. I reached London in the evening on a Saturday. Next day being Sunday everything in London was closed. Either because there were thick

18 curtains in the room or because it was cold, when I woke up I found that it was 10 a.m. This was the first time in my life that I had emulated an Englishman who normally gets up late. I must be up betimes at 5 a.m. This has now advanced to 3 a.m. or so. However, all was well from the next day.

2

In London, at that time there was no institute of archaeology, where teaching and training in all the branches of archaeology were given. I was formally admitted to the University College. Here, the Head of the Department was Professor Bernard Ashmole. He had specialized in Roman Archaeology. The Sumerian language was taught by Sydney Smith of the British Museum. For his lectures we had to go to King's College. A famous professor in the same college taught us Egyptology. Dr R. E. Mortimer Wheeler lectured on excavation at the London Museum, while K. de B. Codrington taught us museology. Indian archaeology was taught by F. J. Richards. He lectured at the School of Oriental Studies as well as guided students for the Ph. D. It was Richards' practice to meet his students at his home at Earl's Court. So I saw him once every week with the assignment he had given me and for future guidance.

After attending a few lectures in Sumerian and Egyptian archaeology, I found that I could not do justice to all the three subjects. For, unlike the practice in India, in London the teachers did not believe in giving formal lecture so much on the special subject they were supposed to teach, but discussed various topics each week informally recommending books to be read on the subject and prescribing an essay which had to be written. And no teacher would allow a student to attend his small, closed session unless this requirement was fulfilled. In a sense, this was the real Upanishadic method of teaching. No formal lectures, as of today, but personal discussion with the pupil was what they thought to be the best form of teaching.

Since Richards gave me each week a different topic to work on, it was not possible for me to fulfil also the requirements of Sidney Smith. So, after a couple of months, I gave up Sumerian and Egyptian studies, though my general interest in those subjects has remained still intact.

3

The weekly sessions with Richards were indeed a revelation; for they soon indicated to me what miracle a teacher could do for a student. Richards was a retired civil servant, having spent a major part of his career in south India. He had written several small papers besides the *Gazetteer of Wynad District* in Kerala. Not only did he gradually make me aware of the problems in Indian archaeology— historic as well as prehistoric—but made me take interest in the people—their names, habits, customs and castes, their professions as well as their culture, music, pottery, weaving, fishing and so on. Thus what I lacked most—geographical, geological, anthropological, and ethnographical background to archaeology—was provided by Richards. What use I made of this background knowledge may be easily noticed in my *Archaeology of Gujarat*, reviewing which the late Professor D. R. Bhandarkar said that I had given "a bird's-eye view of all aspects of Gujarat's history and culture".

It was solely due to Richards that I began taking keen interest in places and personal names in inscriptions as well as the geographical factors in Indian history. The latter aspect was developed by the late Dr B. Subba Rao in his *Personality of India*. However, these aspects did not play a major role in shaping the history of India as I have shown in the second edition of my *Prehistory and Protohistory of India and Pakistan*.

In my first meeting with Richards I told him how I was fascinated by the discoveries at Harappa and Mohenjodaro, a full account of which has recently been published by Marshall in three magnificent volumes. So, he immediately put me on a detailed study of the reports by Hargreaves and Stein. This meant indexing, including drawing each and every design on a potsherd, with a brief description of the potsherds. After I had worked for months on this subject, came the news that Piggott had completed an integrated account of the subject and it would be published soon.

Thwarted in my ambition to do something new about the Indus Valley Civilization, I paid attention to the subject suggested by Codrington—the dynastic study of the medieval monuments. Again I prepared a card index for all the inscriptions listed dynasty-wise by Dr D.R. Bhandarkar and published as an appendix to the *Epigraphia Indica*. After finishing this, the question arose as to which particular dynasty or particular region should be selected. It was just by sheer chance that Gujarat came to be selected. And Gujarat was home-ground to me. After completing the epigraphical survey I turned to the archaeology of Gujarat and its neighbouring areas. This primarily meant an analytical and synthetical study of temple architecture and iconography.

5

About this time (April-May 1935), Dr Mortimer Wheeler, after completing the course of lectures on excavation, had taken us to Maiden Castle and other ancient sites. From one of these field trips one day I had returned at midnight and saw a telegram from India waiting for me. At first I could not make out its purport. For there were a number of "stops". This was the first time I had seen a telegram with no less than three "stops". I wondered whether the Public Service Commission was inviting me to attend an interview for a post of Assistant Superintendent of Archaeology at Simla sometime in June or whether they had previously invited me for an interview which they were now withdrawing. Next day in the earlymorning I showed the telegram to my neighbour Bachubhai Merchant and other friends. They said that it was indeed a call for an interview at Simla.

This invitation, in the midst of my studies and training in England, put me in a great fix. Should I go to India leaving my training and my Ph. D. thesis incomplete ? I consulted Richards, and he felt (not knowing that in all such cases there are Departmental candidates and very often the interview is held only to formalise a decision that has already been taken to select such candidates.) that that was a good opportunity for entering into the Archaeological Survey. Hence he advised me to go. So did my friends in London.

It was also decided that when I returned to India, I should make a field-study of the principal monuments of Gujarat and also undergo training at excavations then being conducted at Chanhudaro, if for some reason I was not selected. This plan was approved of by the university authorities almost immediately, permitting me to remain in India for the next two terms (October-March 1935-36).

This was my first experience of the Public Service Commission. Besides some general questions, the Director-General of Archaeology asked me whether I knew Kharoshthi which I had never studied. So, on my return from Simla, I spent several months learning this script besides continuing my study of temple architecture.

6

At that time Dr Ernst Mackay was excavatingat

Chanhudaro on behalf of the Pennsylvania University Museum, USA. Richards had written to him to permit me to join him and have some training before I returned to England. Mackay agreed but asked me to bring along a tent with me for my stay. Fortunately, these things were easily available on hire at Karachi. So I took one to Nawabsaha from where it was transported on camel-back to Chanhudaro. However, to our great surprise and dismay, when the tent was pitched we found that it had no door flaps. These had been either not supplied or inadvertently left at Karachi. Temporarily, Mackay allowed me to stay in his guest-tent. But I had to vacate it and spend a few days in a partially open tent when Pandit Madho Sarup Vats paid us a visit.

It was then that I heard the discussion about the stratigraphical position of the famous Harappa sandstone torso found by Vats a few years earlier, which both Mackay and Marshall thought could not belong to the Indus Civilization. In the light of the subsequent criticism by Dr Wheeler about the stratification at Mohenjodaro and Harappa, this discussion appeared to be a debate between two ignorant persons. For neither Mackay nor Vats had done real stratigraphical excavations nor had they heard of three dimensional recording of finds. I do remember to have spoken about it to Mackay but he could not even dream of it, because like Marshall he and his assistants recorded "finds" with the help of a Dumpy Level placed at a fixed point. In fact, the way these excavations were being conducted— one overseer looking after a huge trench dug by a couple of hundred labourers – there was not much to be learnt. After I reached Chanhudaro Mackay explained to me the principle of "reversal" according to which the finds from the surface of the area around the mound might not be quite recent but might belong to earlier periods. For it is not improbable that these objects had been washed from the slopes of the mound and have been found lying on the surface!

Mackay also advised me to go to a potter in the nearby village to acquire some idea of his craft. I was then asked to join the pieces of a drain-pipe. While he was not in the field, Mackay would then prepare index cards for each antiquity. This gave me some idea of how to describe an antiquity and how very necessary it was to have a separate antiquity card for each find. Besides such activities there was nothing much to do in the field. This was in direct contrast to what Wheeler had taught us and what he afterwards taught the young and old archaeologists of Indian universities and of the Archaeological Survey of India. So, after spending some three weeks, I left Chanhudaro. On my way back I spent three days at Mohenjodaro which at that time was under the care of K.N. Puri.

Though I did not learn much, my trip to Sind gave me a first-hand idea of the region. As it happened, this turned out to be my first and last visit to Sind. Had I not gone to Sind I would not have been able to see the magnificent site of Mohenjodaro, and the smaller sites like Chanhudaro. I was not much fascinated by Mackay's methods nor by the training he gave. Mackay also thought that I was no good as a field-archaeologist and that I appeared indifferent to field-work. He even reported to that effect to the Public Service Commission when I again appeared for an interview after completing my Ph. D. in London. However, in retrospect and in fairness to Dr Mackay, I would say that while he was not quite wrong, he was also not wholly right. And this I think should be clearly understood. A young man's career is apt to be ruined and it is always advisable to hear what the candidate has to say when an adverse report is made about him by a referee. As far as my own career is concerned, my not being selected for a post in the Archaeological Survey of India was providential. For, had I been selected, probably I could never have had an opportunity to work all over India, publish reports as quickly as I had done and, above all, train more than fifty students and thus remain always fresh and alert.

It was about this time (sometime in October 1934) that my father, worried as he always was about my delicate health, had on the advice of his friend, Bhimji, a solicitor, consulted an astrologer who possessed the *Bhṛigu Saṁhitā*. The difference between ordinary astrologers who cast horoscopes and then tell about the past and future of a person and these *saṁhitas* was that in these *saṁhitas* there are readymade case-histories of all the would-be consultants. These are found written in simple Sanskrit or in a variety of scripts—Tamil, Malyalam and Devanagari—on single sheets, called *pothis*. Since what I have seen are all on paper, none of these could be older than 400 to 500 years. While advising my father, Bhimji had also warned him to be mentally prepared to receive unpleasant predictions. So my father dropped the idea of taking Sarla (my future wife) with him. Instead, he invited one of my solicitor friends, Bhagvat Mehta.

After some preliminary enquiries, which are necessary to decide which particular heroscope should apply to the party concerned, the owner of the *saṁhitā* starts reading. In my case, it was found that when my father would go to consult the *Bhṛigu*, he would be accompanied by a close friend of mine and at that time I would be on the high seas. Then the *saṁhitā* opened my account with the statement that the person born in that conjunction would be an archaeologist—*sa yogo jīrṇashodhakaḥ*. Unfortunately, the sheet of paper on which my father had noted down all the important predictions, is now not available. The one he had sent to me I did not preserve. Hence it is not possible to say which particular predictions have come out right and which have gone wrong. Anyway this astrological prediction did not in any way affect my work either in England or in India. In fact, neither my father nor I believed much in these predictions. For my father had full and implicit faith in God and thus he would always be prepared for all eventualities. He also believed in doing what we had undertaken to do, and not doing anything special suggested by this or that astrologer. Fortunately, Sarla also shared my attitude, so that when we built our house, no *muhurta*, that is, auspicious time, was selected for house construction. Nor was a Brahmin called, for no ceremony was performed at any stage.

7

However, three weeks stay in the dry, cold air of Sind had a salutary effect on my body and mind and I became confident that I could go alone to any part of India. As a result, I planned my own tour of the ancient sites in Northern Gujarat and Kathiawar. At that time, there were no hotels or buses there. So, one had to stay with friends in a city or a village and travel by a cart, or a hackney-carriage (*tonga*), or a private car. I went first to Mount Abu and from there to Siddhapur and Patan, and studied all the important temples mentioned by James Burgess. Then off I went to Junagadh, Girnar and Somnath. On the return journey I stopped at Rajkot with a view to going to Than. Here I was to be the guest of an ex-*dewan* of several states in Kathiawar. He had sent his secretary to receive me at the station who not finding me in the first or second class compartments had returned home. Meanwhile I hired a *tonga* and reached his house. The ex-*dewan* was certainly pleased to see me but was dissatisfied because he had expected me to travel in a class higher than the lowest, being his guest. So as long as I was his guest he made me travel second. The ex-*dewan* also advised me not to go to Dhank because it was supposed to be infested with dacoits. However, when I impressed upon him the necessity of visiting this out-of-the-way place so that I could study the rock-cut sculptures he relented but insisted that I should hire a private car. I paid Rs. 30 which was quite a fortune at that time to be invested for a jaunt. However, the purpose of my visit was more than fulfilled. My studies showed that the sculptures here were not Buddhist but affiliated to Jain faith and probably sculpted in the Gupta period. I, therefore, wrote an article on the subject which was published in the *Journal of the Royal Asiatic Society*, London.

From Dhank I went to Junagadh. Here I was the guest of the ex-*dewan*'s friend who was a lawyer. On the day I reached his house he and his entire family had to go out to attend a marriage dinner. Thus I was passed on from one host to another. Here, to my great surprise, I found unboiled milk being served at dinner. We in cities had been brought up on boiled milk. At Junagadh I met accidentally Shri Shambhuprasad Desai who was then the *vahivatdar* (collector) of Junagadh. He took keen interest in my work, and the fact that I was travelling alone to study all these monuments aroused his admiration. As a typical Kathiawari, he told me that as long as I was in his State (that is, Junagadh), I was to be his guest, and that I would not be allowed to spend a farthing. Thus in his hospitable company I visited Somnath and other sites with great ease. During this tour, I took several photographs with my friend Bachubhai Merchant's camera—a Zeiss Ikon —for the first time in my life. I had never handled a camera before. To my great relief and joy I found that most of the photographs were good enough.

8

It was time for me to return to London and prepare the thesis. This I did, and also participated in the excavations at Maiden Castle. The training was brief, lasting just about a month or so but it was of immense importance to my future career. I learnt here, not only what was stratigraphical digging and drawing of a section and three-dimensional recording of finds (though the finds in my small trench were negligible), but was also made aware of the necessity of minute-to-minute supervision of the trench under one's charge for I was told that at any moment the layer might change and this has to be noted as early as possible. Above all, it removed whatever compunction I had about manual labour. Wheeler disliked any participant who showed the slightest dislike for man ual labour. In fact, when my Bengali colleague said that he had not gone to Maiden Castle to lift stones, he was advised to quit. For Maiden Castle excavation Wheeler engaged not more than two labourers. All the manual work was done by voluntary labour, by young students and retired persons. I also saw how Dr Wheelerinvited the Press and the public to visit his excavations and help him in whatever way they could. Not only was the excavation at Maidan Castlea passport for me to conduct independent excavations in India, butit also showed me how an excavation could be organized without government help with limited funds and voluntary labour.

Returning from Maiden Castle I completed my thesis and submitted it to the university sometime early in December. The *viva* followed. I was to deliver a public lecture at the University College based on my thesis to be presided over by Dr. Stella Kramrisch, the well-known Indologist. We had advertised the lecture on the college notice-board but nobody turned up. There were several slides prepared by Professor Ashmole from my negatives. To my great surprise he showed the slides and he was the only person in the audience besides the President. At the end, Dr Kramrish asked me several questions which I answered, I think, satisfactorily. The one particular question which I still remember at this distance of time (after 40 years) was about the comparison that I had made in my lecture (and also in my thesis) about the styles in the treatment of human, animal and geometric figures in different temples. Such a comparison alones, I said in my lecture, could bring out the regional peculiarity of each set of dynastic monuments. I have consistently followed this method in all my studies of historic, protohistoric and prehistoric archaeology. While no

28   final and definite conclusion can be reached from such a comparison, nevertheless it helps both the writer and the reader to get a view of the subject in a much broader perspective. I know that some scholars regard this as far-fetched but I find it a very rewarding and fascinating exercise.

While returning home I visited Louvre in Paris and the museum in Berlin and Munchen. In the Museum fur Volkerkunde in Berlin I saw a seated gold figure in *Ūrdhvamedhra*, exactly as in the figure of Lakulīśa which became the theme of a small article I wrote for the *Indian Historical Quarterly*. What I admired most during my visits to these museums, was the willingness of the authorities to allow you to photograph the objects of art and to supply the required photographs at a pinch, a facility which we in India miss even today.

9

I landed in Bombay in January 1937. No job awaited me. Twice I appeared before the Public Service Commission, once in Delhi and the second time at Simla, but each time, though I was the best qualified candidate, I was placed third. This naturally disappointed me, my father and my uncle. They advised me to attend the courts with them because I had already taken the *sanad* in 1931.

But I abhorred the very idea. Instead, I resumed my habit of giving tuitions, giving honorary lectures to the B.A. and M.A. students at the St. Xavier's College and regularly visiting the Royal Asiatic Society of Bombay from 11 a.m. to 6 p.m. Here I revised my thesis for the press for which the London University had given a grant of £50. In addition, on the recommendation of my teacher, Sir V.T. Krishnamachari, the *dewan* of Baroda, gave Rs. 5,000 towards its publication.

While this routine work was going on, the

of Wales Museum built a new epigraphical
gallery. Here a number of stone inscriptions were
exhibited for the first time. So Shri G.V. Acharya,
the curator of the archaeological section, invited me
to edit these. Thus I spent a great deal of time deci-
phering no less than eight Śilahāra inscriptions, and
a large stone inscription of Mahamud Begada of
Gujarat.

Palaeography and epigraphy cannot be mastered
by reading either Būhler or Ojha. One must have
an opportunity to read the original and if one is
conscientious enough, hardworking and patient, one
learns to decipher an inscription. The inscription of
Mahamud Begada took me several months to decipher. It was like a cross-word puzzle. Some general
knowledge about the subject one must have. The
rest comes by patient and painstaking effort.

I also worked at the Indian Historical Research
Institute, St. Xavier's College. Here I had already
prepared a catalogue of the pottery excavated by Fr
Heras from Vala in Saurashtra. Though I had in-
dexed and copied all the pottery mentioned by
Marshall, Mackay, Stein, and Hargreaves, this was
the first time that I had an opportunity to handle
pottery physically.

I also catalogued the large collection of Jaina
images in stone and bronze. This also was an excit-
ing piece of work. My models were the works of Professor Norman Brown and Dr Ananda K. Coomara-
swamy. The catalogue was published with a
short introduction in the *New Indian Antiquary* in its
special *festschrift*. At this Institute I found some Kush-
ana, Punchmarked, and tribal coins. I prepared
casts of these coins and wrote on them in the *Numis-
matic Supplement*. Later this experience enabled me
to tackle a large collection of Punch-marked coins
which I had bought for a song from Nagari, near
Chitor.

Thus, in all the traditional branches of historical archaeology, I had opportunities to gain some experience and also to make some original contribution, all without receiving any formal teaching. I learnt by efforts only.

At this time one Nathalal Shah brought to me a beautiful gold-leaf illustrated manuscript of *Bhaktārṇava Stotra*. This MS. was said to be in the possession of Jagat Sheth of Calcutta. Nathalal wanted to sell this—preferably abroad and wanted me to write about it so that it could be given publicity. I was thus introduced to miniature painting and wrote an article in the *Illustrated Weekly of India*, sometime in 1938.

Though I found no remunerative employment after my return from London in 1937, I was not "vegetating", as some of my colleagues thought I did. I had utilized my time well in mastering architecture, sculpture and iconography besides acquiring a fairly good knowledge of the problems of epigraphy, palaeography, and numismatics.

However, my knowledge and experience were of no consequence to the members of the Public Service Commission in Bombay, who while interviewing me for the post of assistant professor said that my *forte* was archaeology and I was no good at teaching history. The Public Service Commission at Allahabad was indeed very much impressed by my work and experience but the U.P. Government deliberated for more than a year and ultimately appointed the late Dr V. S. Agrawala. And who would say that their choice was not right? Meanwhile, the Bombay Municipality had selected me for the post of the Curator of their Museum in the Victoria Gardens. But when they learnt that I had applied for better posts elsewhere, they withdrew the offer. Thus I continued to be without a job.

What possibly helped me to find a job in 1939
(according to the commonly held Indian belief) was
my marriage in May 1938, nearly five and a half
years after my engagement to Sarla in 1933. Though
I was against celebrating it on a grand scale, I got
married in one of the finest and choicest places in
Bombay i.e. Madhav Bag, V. P. Road. This place was
opposite to our old residence, Khakhar Building and
I had witnessed many marriages taking place there
but never dreamt or thought that I would be one
day married there. This was on May 4, 1938. Next
year I was appointed an examiner in matriculation
examination—a work which fetched me Rs. 300 or
so. Hence I thought of visiting Kashmir with my
wife with the small sum of money that I had earned.
Holiday return tickets were then available for a
single fare only and I bought two tickets.

On our way at Lahore station I bought a copy
of the *Civil and Military Gazette*. In the advertisement
columns I found that the Deccan College Postgra-
duate and Research Institute had advertised for
teaching posts. So on reaching Srinagar, I wrote to
my father to get me an application form. I think I
also wrote to the Deccan College. The form was
duly received and I posted the application from
Pahlgam. I did not know then that at Pahlgam
after a few years I would discover Stone Age
tools.

A curious incident happened at Srinagar. We
were staying in a Sikh hotel overlooking one of the
Bridges. One day a tall, old man, dressed like a
sanyāsī, came and asked for Rs. 25. This was too
large a sum of money to be given away at that time
or even now. So, I expressed my inability to meet
with his request. He did not get angry. On the
contrary he left saying that very soon I would get a
post carrying a salary of Rs. 400 per month.

I had completely forgotten this incident but recalled it when I found that the post at Pune for which I was selected carried a fixed salary of Rs. 400 *per mensem*. So when I got the job I enquired about that astrologer-*cum*-beggar at Srinagar, but the manager, who had become our friend by that time, informed me that he had never seen that man again. This small incident is of some significance because the salary offered at the Deccan College was quite unusual. Normally Class I posts at that time were in the grade of Rs. 300-25-350—Rs. 630, but I was given a start of Rs. 400.

After returning to Bombay, I was first interviewed for the post of an Assistant Professor in history by the Public Service Commission. I have already referred to the result of the interview. My major hope was, therefore, the post of Professor of Proto-Indian and Ancient Indian History at the Deccan College at Poona, now renamed as Pune. Initially it was for a period of eight months only, after which there was to be a fresh selection. Moreover, it was doubtful if a Gujarati would be selected in this stronghold of Maharashtrians. More important was the fact that Dr B. A. Salator was one among the candidates to be interviewed. He was already a professor and he had, I learnt afterwards, a hand in the drafting of the Constitution of the Deccan College.

However, I was full of confidence when I found that the Committee consisted of Dr D. R. Gadgil, Prof D.V. Potdar, Prof Karmarkar and Prof P.V. Kane, and possibly Prof R.P. Patwardhan. Except Kane, I had not known anybody, and saw them for the first time when I went to the interview. Between Salator and myself, their choice naturally fell on me because my experience and qualifications suited the post of Prof of Proto-Indian History. Dr Salator was a specialist in Mediaeval Indian History. Secondly, as I learnt later from both Kane and Potdar that the Board was impressed by the fact that I had some

The Committee asked me if I would accept Readership, if it was decided to institute a Professorship only either in Mediaeval or Maratha History. I flatly refused. But within a few days the appointment letter for the post of a Professor came from the Deccan College. The fact that the appointment was for eight months made me and my father a little apprehensive. Why not wait for the post of Curator in the Prince of Wales Museum in Bombay which carried a higher salary?

When we were in this dilemma, Fr. Heras gave me a clear and decisive advice. He said that, though the post at Pune was of a temporary nature I need not worry. Once I was there, I was bound to do good work and nobody would think of driving me out. Secondly, at Pune I would "live"; while in a museum one was likely to become a "fossil" with fewer opportunities of coming into contact with young students. The advice turned out to be fully right as my subsequent career unfolded. So, on August 17 I left Bombay by the first train and reached Pune at about 12 noon. At that time one could hire a *tonga* (hackney carriage) for the whole day. For a rupee and a half I hired one and entered the vast portals of the Deccan College with its magnificent Gothic towers.

Three

Deccan College

> *1. Deccan College 2. Dr Katre 3. First Pupils
> 4. Discovery of Megaliths 5. K. N. Dikshit
> 6. Gujarat Expedition 7. Food Problem 8. Miraculous
> Cure 9. Sarla Joins us 10. Chatterjee and
> Krishnaswami.*

AT the Deccan College I met Dr S.M. Katre,
Dr Iravati Karve, C.R. Sankaran, Chand Shaikh,
Dr R.G. Harshe, Kanitkar, T.S. Shejwalkar for the
first time. Except Dr Katre I did not correspond
with any of them earlier. Next day, or perhaps the
same day, Dr V.M. Apte joined us. He acted as
the Director just for one day because it was said
that he belonged to Class II in the Bombay Government Service and, hence, could not be appointed as a
Director. The actual reason was never known, nor did
any of us care to know. However, his not remaining
the Director was indeed providential. For, had
Dr Apte continued as the Director, I am sure, we
would all have been strangulated, head and foot,
by rules and regulations and the world would never
have witnessed the flowering of a young institution
as a centre of research and learning.

All of us, excepting Shejwalkar, were fairly young
who had never seen the seamy side of life. Above
all, we were devoted to research in our chosen fields.
We were all, therefore, thankful to God for the
opportunity He had given us, though we knew in

contrast to conditions prevailing elsewhere in the universities, our salary was not only modest but fixed without the benefit of pension, provident fund or gratuity. A very modest provident fund was given to us later. However, the pecuniary loss was more than compensated by the immense possibilities that we had for putting our plans for work in practice. Originally we were all supposed to do some field research, but owing to the war-time condition in 1941 Dr Katre and Sankaran were obliged to give up their plans of work in the Nilgiris. The former then planned to compile the *Dictionary of Inscriptional Sanskrit* and the latter paid attention to Instrumental phonetics. And thus only Dr Iravati Karve and myself were left in the field. How each one of us developed is by now well-known.

2

Our first Director, Dr I. J.S. Taraporewala, and also Dr Katre, our Director from 1942 to 1970, allowed freedom to each one of us to plan and execute our schemes. Naturally while doing our tasks each one of us would establish independent contacts with scholars, institutions as well as patrons of learning in India and outside. If due to these contacts with persons and institutions funds were made available for our individual or departmental schemes, Dr Katre never objected. He never insisted that he should be consulted first. In the same way, he did not think that we should confine our work to the four corners of Maharashtra or to this or that subject. Neither did he nor any of us feel that students outside Maharashtra should not be given scholarship or sizarship if the students deserved it. Non-interference in the work of others. faith in the competence of the individual as well as complete freedom to plan and execute one's scheme of research within the means at our disposal were mainly responsible for the rapid development of the Deccan College.

36   I should like to mention an instance of how
Dr Katre took a very sympathetic view of my situation, so that I was not put to unnecessary loss and
hardship. In 1947-48 my landlord harassed us so
much that my wife and I had to leave immediately
for Bombay locking our house on the Jungli Maharaj
Road until some alternate accommodation was
available in Pune. I, therefore, went to Bombay
and worked in the Asiatic Society. All those days
I was not at Pune were not counted as leave but as
"on duty". Where on earth do we find a Director
who had so much of understanding ? Of course,
none of us, excepting Shejwalkar misused this trust
and confidence placed in us. Though he was a great
scholar, extremely well-read and well-informed, he
would not write or even dictate what he knew and
thought. Thus he did not fulfil one-tenth of the
promise he made every year. Consequently his
services had to be discontinued and it was left to
me to refuse him extension after he was super-
annuated. Of course, Dr. Katre could never have
taken this most unpleasant step, because his motto
in life was *to live and let live*. With all his good qualities Shejwalkar was a misanthrope and would therefore always over emphasize the darker side of a man.

     Dr Katre had another rare quality. He loved
good printing and had spent sometime in learning the
various aspects of this art. Not only did he love
printing, but also took great delight in printing our
research papers as well as of others with meticulous
care. How he did this within the small publication
grant that we had, I had never cared to enquire till
I became the Director in 1970. It is because of his
initiative that a large number of publications which
the Deccan College has to its credit today was
made possible particularly its several well-illustrated
monographs on archaeological subjects. I can say
that throughout my stay at the Deccan College
I have always felt that it is not the rules and regulations that go to make an institution great. What
makes it expand is the trust and confidence the

head of the institute places in his fellow-workers and, 37
above all, sympathy and a desire to help them and
not to hinder their work.

3

Long before I joined the Deccan College, I had
planned to reconstruct the history of India by a
study of the Puranas and also of Sanskrit literature
testing my conclusions in the light of archaeology.
My teaching career started with a couple of students
who came to me within a week of my joining the
institute for the Ph.D. The subjects were ready at
hand. Whom to select for which branch of study
would depend naturally upon the students' aptitude
and background. To A.V. Naik I suggested "Archaeology of the Deccan." To D.R. Patil was given the
"Cultural History in the Vāyu Purāṇa". Both of them
did excellently well. Before Patil began the study
of the *Vāyu Purāṇa*, I asked him to study the Gupta
inscriptions and collect all the allusions to the
puranic stories. Such a study would give us a firm
foundation for dating that much portion at least in
the various Puranas. Naik had no difficulty, as he
would often tell me. A model was set before him by
my *Archaeology of Gujarat*. Not only did he follow my
model but made a study of many more monuments
which he came across in his field-work for which we
gave research grants to students. But before he undertook this work I had taken him and other students
during the *Diwali* holidays to the Prince of Wales
Museum in Bombay and taught them the elements
of iconography. Later, they were taken to the caves
at Karla, Bhaja, and Junnar. At Junnar they were
taught how to take impressions of stone inscriptions.
All these I called as "Study Tours". During these
tours we had to pay for our own expenses—food as
well as travelling—from our own pockets. Later,
similar but more extensive tours were undertaken
in the Nizam's Dominions. Thus, before 1941, my
students and I had first-hand acquaintance with all
the important monuments of the Satavahanas, the

Chalukyas, the Rastrakutas, the Yadavas and their contemporaries in Andhra Pradesh, Karnataka, Maharashtra, and Tamil Nadu.

For my own research I first began by studying the *Poona Gazetteer*, studying side by side the inscriptions of the Gurjara-Pratiharas with a view to undertaking a tour in search of their monuments and studying them as well as I could. These were barely known. The late Professor D.R. Bhandarkar had noticed a few of them when he was the Superintendent of the Western Circle in the Archaeological Survey of India. So when I consulted him, he wrote to me that I would have to rough out, meaning thereby that I would have to go from place to place in Rajasthan to locate them. Naturally adequate groundwork must precede before undertaking such a study.

4

Meanwhile an intensive study of the *Poona Gazetteer* revealed that there was a ruined temple, perhaps of the Yadava Period, in the jungle at Pur, at a distance of some eight to ten miles from Junnar, the nearest village. And at Bhavsari some eight miles from Pune on the Pune-Nasik road, are to be found megalithic stone-circles. Though I had no occasion to study or see the true south Indian megaliths, this brief reference struck me as worthy of investigation. So, early in November, Naik, Patil and I went to Bhavsari, and made detailed enquiries, as I was taught to do by Richards—a line of enquiry which is further explained in *Notes and Queries in Anthropology*—a guidebook published by the Anthropological Institute of London. Later the monuments were fully surveyed and a report in the form of a paper was published in the bulletin of the Deccan College.

As I have pointed out elsewhere, these are not true megaliths of the south Indian type, but only memorial stones erected in memory of the dead but exactly modelled after typical megalithic structures such as menhirs, dolmens and stone alignments. I was sorry to find that there was no scope for excavation, as these monuments rose right from the rock surface, and there were no debris or other constructional features which we could study to ascertain the dates of these monuments.

It is a pity that pseudo-archaeologists not knowing what actually obtains at Bhavsari have criticised me for not carrying out excavations there and other adjacent sites. Though the Bhavsari monuments are not true megaliths, those from Western Maharashtra do indicate the influence of the monuments of Karnataka which are true megaliths. Excellent proof has recently been obtained at Pimpalsuti, near Inamgaon, and other places in the Pune district.

The exploration at Pur was far from easy. We went to Junnar by an old Ford car, no other conveyance being available then. But when we proceeded and reached Rajur, we found that there was not even a cart track and the region being hilly, a cross-country drive was out of question. So we left the car at Rajur and decided to walk upto Nanaghat in one day and returned after a strenuous walk of some sixteen miles. Since we had left our beddings at Junnar, we slept on the bare ground in our field-clothes enjoying the hospitality of a villager. Next day, we went to Pur. The temple was located in the heart of the jungle—a good and true specimen of Yadava art and architecture. Naturally a fully documented article was published in our *Bulletin*.

5

These small discoveries, at and near Pune, opened the eyes of the then Director General of Archaeology, Rao Bahadur K.N. Dikshit. He was convinced that not only was I capable of writing a thesis based on published material, but I could discover new finds as well and also undergo strenuous and hazard-

ous exploration. In fact, he asked his Superintendent at Pune why these had not been noticed by
him during the years of his tenure. It would not be
an exaggeration if I pun on the word 'Bhavsari' like
the old Sanskrit poets and say that my *bhava* (life,
career) was made smooth (*sara*) by Bhavsari. Soon
after Rao Bahadur Dikshit who had once spurned
and ridiculed my offer to undertake exploration in
Sind, (since I knew the area) sent for me on his next
visit to Pune in August or September, 1940. What
had happened earlier needs a brief narration. In
June or July that year he had given a lecture on
the Indus Civilization at the Bhandarkar Oriental
Research Institute and said that the Survey was
compelled to abandon any further exploration in
Sind because N.G. Majumdar was brutally murder-
ed in cold blood in the Dadu district. Next morning,
I went to see off Dikshit at the railway station who
was leaving by the "Deccan Queen." I expressed
my willingness to continue the work left unfinished
by the late Majumdar. He told me that I should
mind my own business.

When I went to his office at Sangam in Pune, he
asked me if I had read *Notes* by Bruce Foote and
whether I was aware of the problem he had raised
about the hiatus between the palaeolithic and neolithic finds in Gujarat. I told him that not only had I
seen the book but had also made extensive notes
and prepared a map showing all the sites mentioned
by Foote. He then said, "Who asked you to do all
this?" "Richards", I replied. He then asked me
whether I would be prepared to lead an expedition to
Gujarat with a view to solving the problem raised by
Foote. "I am perfectly willing", I said, "but I should
be assisted by a geologist, a palaeontologist and a
surveyor draftsman." He promised to send them and
asked me to get ready.

Though I had made notes from Foote's book
and had also probably seen a few palaeolithic sites
in England, I had never studied prehistory nor

handled palaeolithic, microlithic and neolithic finds. 41

But when the Deccan College was shifted to the
Jeejibhoy Castle, the late Dr Iravati Karve asked
me to teach European prehistory. At that time she
was the only "recognised teacher" in sociology and
therefore she was required to teach all the four or
eight papers in this subject. For a single teacher,
this was certainly a burden. So one day she placed
in my hands G.G. MacCurdy's *Human Origins* so
that I could teach prehistory and share some of her
burden. These volumes, though published in 1923
were excellent for an introduction to European prehistory Even now, after fifty-five years, I would
still recommend his book to a novice. MacCurdy
has explained very systematically with necessary
illustrations all about the Ice Age as well as the
various sites and the development of the Stone Age
which a beginner should know.

So I began to study his book systematically,
preparing drawings and charts for my sociology
students. I found that this was not enough. The
lectures on prehistory, if they are to be properly
understood, have to be illustrated. So with the help
of the photo-registry office, I got 35 mm films made
of the entire book as well as Marshall's *Indus Civilization* and De Terra and Paterson's *Ice Age and
Associated Human Remains*. The last book had then
just been published. It made a very heavy reading,
particularly for a non-specialist like me. But I had
developed a method of reading by which even a
most difficult book could be mastered. So, when
V. D. Krishnaswamy joined me and discussed with
me the plans about our expedition, I had all the
book-knowledge one could have. I had never seen
a river section in the field nor had handled a palaeolithic find. Nor had I any occasion to consult one-
inch-to-mile survey maps. Fortunately, Prof R.P.
Patwardhan, who was asked to organize the library
just before the Deccan College started the Research
Institute, had purchased all the one-inch maps then
available. These came in very handy for planning

Rao Bahadur Dikshit had appointed, as desired by me, two experts—one was Krishnaswamy a geologist and the other was Dr B. K. Chatterjee, a palaeontologist. Then there was a young draftsman-surveyor, besides the official photographer, Devi Dayal and Sadardin, the peon. The team was to be assisted by A.S. Gadre, who was then the Assistant Director of Archaeology, Baroda State. He was supposed to make arrangements for our accommodation and also to arrange labourers to do the digging while we were in his jurisdiction.

6

As the leader of the expedition I had to arrange all those equipments that we would require in the field—tools (pickaxes, hammers and knives), packing boxes and several kinds of bags for collection and storage of finds, various kinds of labels and stationery. Bags and containers that I had purchased could be easily packed in "camel-back" trunks. These were the legacies of the First World War which my brother-in-law, Major Dr K.V. Tolat had preserved, and which he gave me as soon as he knew of my predicament. He also offered me his military jackets which had four large pockets, a khaki coat with large brass buttons, breaches and *puttee*. Of course, all these had to be altered because these were now to be worn by a person whose weight was just 90 lbs., whereas the person for whom these were bought originally should have weighed at least 140 lbs.

When I donned my uniform, Krishnaswami, who seemed to take fancy to formal dress, said, "Now you look like a real leader." It is indeed unfortunate that we have given up such formidable but useful clothes, because one appeared "over-dressed", as Zeuner remarked when he first saw me in my military garb. Be that as it may, I could keep a pocket diary, purse, camera stand (folding) and all

inside those capacious pockets. The breeches again
enabled me to walk, run, climb and squat anywhere
I liked without any difficulty. The narrow drainpipe—
now out of fashion—or the wide bell-bottom trousers
—now in vogue—cannot have those advantages.
In fact, these are a positive nuisance in any kind of
expedition, so also shirts with small pockets. I
have seen boys and girls cutting sorry figures with
their drainpipes in our Kerala tour of 1974 or the
Malvan exploration, near Surat, in March 1975.

Particularly difficult was the problem of food.
We would be far away from any habitation and could
not, therefore, think of any hotel or any other place
where we could have our food. We had to be self-suffi-
cient and be prepared for all eventualities as in the
army. Rao Bahadur Dikshit had little idea of this.
For him as well as the officers of the Archaeological
Survey, there would be special officers who would
take charge of all the camp equipment. So he repeatedly sent me telegrams as to when I would go to
the field, and was so impatient that he ordered the
rest of the party to assemble at Vijapur, the *Taluka*
headquarters in North Gujarat. Though I had
personally purchased with my own funds all the
equipment and had arranged the kinds of bags and
stationery that we would require, according to the
advice given by Krishnaswamy, my difficulty was
that I had no cook of my own at the Deccan
College. I wondered who would cook for such a
large party while in the field, if I did not take one
along with me from Pune or Bombay. In the excavations organized by the Survey, I found that there
was no common kitchen. Each one of the officers
looks after himself aided by a servant. I was not
used to this luxury, nor could I think of it. In our
camps at Gujarat and later at other places all of us,
irrespective of our status, we shared the same food
and paid for the food in proportion to our salary or
allowance. Thus there was true socialism in our
camp. Since no peon of the Deccan College was
willing to go with me to Gujarat, my father lent me

our family servant from Bombay. But the cook had
to be hired.

7

These small details, otherwise insignificant, have
been mentioned because it was for the first time that
so many people, from different parts of India, were
brought together, under one head, who himself not
being a Government officer, had to organize an
expedition besides taking care of academic and scientific work and other personal needs. I had fortunately thought of all our needs including such small
details as containers for storing oil, ghee and milk as
well as tiffin-carriers for carrying our lunch on the
field, hurricane lanterns and all.

Food, however, remained the problem. Our cook
was a Gujarati whereas in our party there were a
south Indian, a Bengali, one Pathan, one Kathia-
wadi and two Maharashtrians and two more from
Uttar Pradesh. It was impossible to satisfy the mis-
cellaneous tastes of all. Those from U.P. were accustomed to eating food cooked in *ghee*, whereas the
south Indian preferred liquid food, and the Bengali
would want his pound of fish. On the very first day,
December 7, not satisfied with the food, some members wanted me to chuck out the cook. I flatly refused. There was a minor mutiny. But I stuck though
there was danger of losing an expert. I was prepared
to bear his loss but not that of the cook. Without
him we would not be able to move an inch on the
banks of the Sabarmati and our expedition would
be a total failure.

8

My firmness paid and next day we visited the
classic site of Hirpura and made a few discoveries of
flakes in the cemented gravel. I duly reported this,
mentioning the names of the finders to Rao Bahadur
Dikshit. I had taken my own portable typewriter

on which I would write the daily reports. At Hirpura we also discovered a few microliths on a sandy mound. Hence it was carefully dug under my personal super-vision. Then the party moved on to Pedhamli. Un-fortunately, during the night I had a severe attack of diarrohea, which for some reason or other would not abate and so I was left alone in the school-room where we had been staying. Unfortunately I did not have any medicine and the village had no doctor. Only a miracle cured me. The village headman knew of a *vaidya*-cum-masseur. He was summoned. He passed his palm over my abdomen and said that nothing was wrong with me except that there was some glandular displacement because of working up and down the river-side which could be cured by a little massage ! And so he did ! He then said that after this massage I should take *shira* (wheat flour mixed with sugar and cooked in *ghee*). Not only did this strange treatment cure me, but gave me strength enough to walk up to Pedhamli, a distance of a few miles from Hirapur and join the party there. Here a large collection of handaxes, cleavers and other tools had been made in Luhar Nala and other locali-ties. And with this vast collection I gloriously walked back to Vijapur.

Meanwhile our party faced another obstacle in our field-work. Since there were no metalled roads but only tracks, and that too on a sandy surface, it was not possible to engage a vehicle — neither a bus nor a truck or even a hackney carriage, *tonga* would be willing to take us. Our photogra-pher, who had never before participated in such a field-work and was used to "still" photography only, insisted that we must engage *tongas* to reach our haven. He said that no commander could ignore the wishes of his army, and quoted some incidents from the life of Nepoleon Bonaparte. So we gave his suggestion a try but found it so time-consuming and inconvenient, that we had to give it up at last. Thus we were left to walking leaving our camp at 7 a.m. with lunch packed in tiffin-carriers and

46 return sometime in the evening. This meant walking daily a distance of 15 to 20 miles. And then we and the Government experts and appointees learnt that the daily allowance would go up if the distance covered was more than 20 miles. The allowance was ridiculously low—the experts getting just a rupee and the attendants two annas per day. This was hardly sufficient to meet the cost of two square meals a day including a cup of tea. Somehow we managed, because we ran our mess on a socialist basis, I paying the maximum.

9

After my short, but severe, illness my wife joined the expedition. She participated in all our explorations, walking with her sandals on stones and sands miles on end. Naturally when she discovered anything—a palaeolith or a microlith—I included her name in my weekly reports. To this Rao Bahadur objected saying that she was not an official member of the expedition. However, when both Krishnaswamy and Chatterjee had gone to Delhi to attend the interview of the post of Assistant Superintendent of prehistory, and Gadre was engaged on one mound, my wife was the only assistant and collaborator on the main Andhario mound at Langhanj. What we found we noted carefully and packed it up separately trying it neatly with a thread, rubber bands being then unknown. And I must say Sarla had an eye for locating the microliths. Usually it was from the ratholes that she ferreted out these tiny tools.

10

The atmosphere in our comp completely changed when Chatterjee and Krishnaswamy rejoined me at Ahmedabad. They alleged that they were badly treated, when they were in Delhi. To the Director-General of Archaeology, their knowledge of prehistory was of no use. He wanted a person well-versed in the Indus Civilisation and so K.N. Puri,

who was already in the Department was selected.
Both Chatterjee and Krishnaswami felt that they had
been let down by Dikshit. By offering them these
temporary appointments of prehistorians, he had
raised false hopes in their minds. On reaching
Ahmedabad they said that they would leave the expedition. I requested them not to do so and wanted
them to complete the remaining part of the expedition, namely the survey of the Orsang and Hiran at
Bahadurpur in Central Gujarat.

I must say that Krishnaswami was very helpful.
He had helped me in planning at Pune and co-operated excellently in planning the day-to-day surveys
by studying the survey maps. And it was his planning
that had helped us finally to go to Hadol in the
upper reaches of the Sabarmati. But he refused to
co-operate with us any further after his debacle in
the Delhi interview. This certainly came as a shock
to me because he was the most experienced prehistorian of our team. He had previously worked
with De Terra and Paterson and also had his training
under Burkitt at Cambridge. Chatterjee was of little
use. When I asked him to give me his field-notes he
promptly gave me a blank note-book: Under the
circumstances, the question of preparing the report
could not be entertained and all the finds had to be
transported to Delhi without our valuation.

Four

Experience of Prehistory

1. *Becoming a Prehistorian* 2. *Godavari Survey*
3. *Microlithic Man* 4. *Kolhapur* 5. *Langhnaj
Again* 6. *Deshpande and Subbarao* 7. *Nasik*
8. *Deccan College: Home of Early Man* 9. *Dr
Deo and Dr Ansari* 10. *Nevasa* 11. *Testing of
Puranic Legends* 12. *Maheshwar and Maratha
Architecture* 13. *Nathadvara: Rajasthan prehistory.*

HOWEVER, on returning to Pune I recovered my
confidence, and requested Rao Bahadur Dikshit to
send the finds so that I could start working on them.
This he did promptly. Though it was Summer
vacation I used to go to the Institute at 8 a.m. and
worked there till noon. Side by side I updated my
knowledge by consulting all the latest books on
European prehistory we had at Pune. Then I went
to Madras and studied the entire Foote collection of
microliths, palaeoliths and potsherds from all over
south India. I also wanted to go to Calcutta, but
it was in the throes of war, as the Japanese had
invaded Burma. They were then actually on the
frontiers of India. Intensive study made me a prehistorian. What I produced at the end of two years,
in 1944, is well-known. Burkitt reviewing it in *Nature*
called the book "excellent". Prof. Zeuner felt that the
work I did was very creditable. He told me this in
1948 or thereabout when one day we were reviewing
our work sitting on the bank of the Sabarmati.
Had Krishnaswami remained with me, I really

doubt, if this self development could have been possible for he knew his subject well enough, and naturally it was expected that he would write on the palaeolithic collection, whereas I was expected to devote my attention to the excavated material.

2

When we review the work done in prehistory and protohistory during the last twenty-five years in India, who would deny that I was not instrumental in playing an important role? Mind you, I had no hand, either direct or indirect, in disqualifying either Chatterjee or Krishnaswami. Later when Krishnaswami was appointed the prehistorian in the Survey, somehow he was not allowed to do what he was most fit to do and was shifted to the General line. Anyway, while preparing the report on our Gujarat Expedition, I thoroughly acquainted myself with all the geological reports besides works on European, African and Asiatic prehistory. In one old report I read that large animal fossils had been found at Nandur Madhmeshwar on the Godavari. And I thought to myself if I should not examine this site. So I went with Patil and stayed in a friend's house at Niphad.

Here for the first time I saw a fairly high section in Maharashtra rivers but it was nothing compared to that on the Sabarmati or the Mahi. Moreover, the boulder or pebble conglomerates were missing. However, we did find a few smaller tools made of chert and jasper in a gravel layer. And thus was laid the foundation of the Middle Palaeolithic. Of course, immediately I did not know their real significance. In fact, we were disappointed in not finding large tools—palaeoliths—as in Gujarat. Even this small work was noticed in *Nature*.

Thus from one river valley to another, I went on gathering artefacts. And the Man who had rejected me thrice said that he did not know that I was capable of such hard work and planning my work independently! It may be of interest to note that while many scholars in India and abroad have appreciated both these aspects of my work at the Deccan College, a few have regarded this as nothing but donkey's work. But I may tell them that systematic planning, followed by hard work alone leads to success in any discipline and much more so in archaeology which entails the labour of sifting, collecting, and discovering of material things.

3

Dikshit had no plan of continuing the work in Gujarat. According to him, we had confirmed the existence of a hiatus between the Palaeolithic and the Neolithic in Gujarat. But in any scientific investigation—as also in criminology—one thing leads to another. Particularly this is true of archaeology. So far we had not thought of Man, the author of the palaeoliths and microliths. I discovered him at Langhnaj in an interesting accident. My room in the Jeejeebhoy Castle and later at the Deccan College was always filled with the finds, since I always worked on them when I was not lecturing or doing any other work. On my table at the Jeejeebhoy Castle lay trays of assorted bones from the Langhnaj excavation. The late Dr Karve who took a keen interest in my work would often step into my room to see these bones. Sometime in 1943, while cursorily examining these assorted bones—which I thought were all of animals—she picked up a fragment of a bone and said that the fragment must be of a human skull. Trained as she was by a famous human palaeontologist she got excited. For here was a chance, she said, of finding the Stone Age Man—may be microlithic or mesolithic—but certainly the earliest man in India.

This led to our second Gujarat expedition organised specifically to find out the microlithic Man in Gujarat. Its members were mainly two—Dr Iravati Karve and myself. Rao Bahadur Dikshit had lent

the services of his foreman, Sadar Din. The expedition was financed by a grant from the University of
Bombay. We left for Langhnaj as soon as I completed the report on the first expedition and forwarded
it to Rao Bahadur Dikshit. The results are now
well known. Subsequently we continued the work
for years.

The first human skeleton of the Stone Age Man
was discovered on February 28, 1944. Iravati Karve
was so much pleased that she thought of celebrating
the occasion by offering me a glass of lemon juice.
This did not agree with me not being accustomed to
cold drinks even on a very hot day. Next day, I felt
sick and had an attack of diarrhoea and I was completely run down. And though vomiting stopped,
the diarrhoea continued. With great difficulty we
reached Pune. The weakness in my legs too continued for months. And I wondered whether I would
be able to do any field-work at all. However, a
course of ematine injections restored my health.

4

The lure of Langhnaj once again spurred
Dr Karve and me to work further with still more
spectacular results. Normally, I should have continued to work in prehistory alone. But my general
interest in all aspects of history and the news that
I was a mascot—lucky to find the earliest human
skeletons—had reached Kolhapur through Dr Karve
and the late Dr D.R. Gadgil who was her neighbour.
Secondly, scholars as well as laymen were anxious
that I should do some work—excavation—in Maharashtra. And why not try at Kolhapur if the State
was willing to help financially? Just then, accidentally, a local archaeologist, the late Professor
Kundangar, had found one of the richest hoards of
bronzes in India on the banks of the Panchganga.

I welcomed the opportunity, and asked my
colleague Dr M. G. Dikshit, the Curator of Satara

52 Collection, to join me. Though we began our operation with some fanfare we soon realized that we were really not wanted there. In spite of impediments we continued for more than three months, though at the end we had to return to Pune without the finds because the local archaeologist said that only a few finds could be sent along with us! How can one who is used to writing a full report agree to this absurd condition?

However, this excavation gave me an excellent experience of stratification which I missed at Langhnaj. Besides the various occupation layers I could find that one of the top-most layers was formed when this part of the city was submerged by the Panchganga. My inference very much surprised Rao Bahadur Dikshit who had come to see our excavation. He was, however, convinced when he saw how the layer tapered off towards the city, and that it contained nothing but washed out material and consisted of reddish sticky clay.

This was again a large excavation which yielded many kinds of finds. All these had to be registered, sorted out, and arranged datewise. Since we had no other assistants, these had to be done by Dikshit and myself. I had also undertaken to clean the coins as and when they were found just to acquaint ourselves with the probable dates of the layers that we were digging. Besides, a large stratigraphical excavation gave us a good idea of the pottery of various historical phases—a knowledge indispensable for recognising true prehistoric pottery.

In spite of the opposition from local scholars, we had organized an exhibition of the finds at the close of the excavation. For, I always believed that a work of this kind is not undertaken to win laurels or for writing academic reports, but for educating the public about past.

Back from Kolhapur, I had to organise a bigger
expedition to Gujarat. It was organised with the
funds given by the Sir Dorabjee and Lady Ratan
Tata Trusts in response to an appeal issued by Rao
Bahadur Dikshit. Our main aim was to discover
the layer or layers below which the human skeletons
laid buried at Langhnaj. We had been unable to
discover this in 1944 and 1945, a fact which had
very much disconcerted Dr Mortimer Wheeler, who
had then taken over as the Director-General of
Archaeology in India. Being my former teacher,
he knew that I should not be condemned outright
but expressed surprise that we could not trace the
pit-line and thus ascertain the true stratigraphical
position of the human skeleton.

In this expedition we were not alone. To assist
us came, besides Shaikh (Z.D. Ansari), who had
joined me as a photographer in 1945 at Kolhapur,
Subbarao, who had worked with Wheeler at
Harappa, and Shekhar, who had worked at Arikc-
medu. Thus a strong team of youngmen, had once
again landed at Langhnaj.

Just towards the end, before Wheeler arrived to
inspect our work, Shekhar had devised a very
ingenious method of ascertaining the layer in sandy
medium. Wheeler came and with his methodical
care and skill shaved the section for more than two
hours but was unable to discern any pit line. Then
Shekhar placed a piece of paper at the foot of the
section, and very carefully and slowly went on
scrapping the section, noting at the same time the
change in the colour of the sandy soil falling on the
paper. By this method, at least, a sub-division or
two could be discerned below three feet of the brow-
nish silt. On seeing the results, Wheeler immediately complimented us, and said that he had learnt
something new about stratification. And then he
advised us to dig at Langhnaj according to this

method of stratification. We found that was not possible. So he advised us to write to Professor Zeuner. Thus begun a new phase in Indian Archaeology and my training, in particular in the environment of Man. So once again we went to Gujarat. This time Zeuner taught me something about the red weathering and dry and wet phases. It was Zeuner who had first identified the large teeth of the rhinoceros at Langhnaj, an identification which he later confirmed by studying the shoulder blade. But the hydrochloric acid test by which he had first indicated a wet phase at Langhnaj, he later rejected. Now this season Dr G.G. Mujumdar is making one more attempt to differentiate between the layers by chemical analysis of the sandy soil.

6

Since nothing more could be done at Langhnaj, I stopped going to Gujarat. But soon my attention was drawn to Nasik where a few potsherds had been discovered by M.N. Deshpande, my former pupil who was then the Assistant Superintendent in the Survey.

Deshpande's case is worth narrating. He had enrolled himself under me for Ph.D. in Jainology. I had suggested him this subject because he had obtained a first class in B.A. in ardhamagadhi. Just then Wheeler had started his training school at Taxila, I advised Deshpande to go and attend the school. I also called him to my house on Jangli Maharaj Road, and gave him some idea of stratification and warned him particularly never to shirk any manual labour, because Wheeler was a great taskmaster and would certainly dislike anyone who hated manual work. Deshpande followed these instructions to the latter, and when in one of the field lectures he answered Wheeler's questions to his satisfaction, Deshpande became one of Wheeler's favourite students. Wheeler himself sent him an application form for one of the studentships and hardly the period of studentship was over when he was appointed an Assistant Superintendent! There were similar other cases. Once Wheeler liked some one, his appointments and promotions followed in quick succession. But it must be admitted his was not pure fancy.

Wheeler was a good and excellent judge of men, of their work and of their merit. Thus he advised me not to send Subbarao to an interview in the Public Service Commission. And he was right. Subbarao had developed a peculiar inferiority complex because of his physical defect. He also felt so much nervous before approaching his superior that he would go round and round his room. But he become a great scholar and field-worker. It was indeed a pity that he died so early.

Anyway, it was with the help of Wheeler that I took up the Neolithic problem in south India. Subbarao was sent to me by Dr Radha Kumud Mukherjee of Lucknow University with a suggestion that he should work on the Satavahanas. Since considerable work had been done on this theme, I asked Subbarao whether he would like to work on the Neolithic of Bellary. The subject involved considerable fieldwork, and would have to be followed by a small excavation. This was before Wheeler had dug at Brahmagiri. To my great surprise and joy, Subbarao, though otherwise shy and nervous, did an excellent job of it. And it was done truly single handed. Not only he had lost his right hand, but also he got no assistance from me. Just when I was to leave for Bellary to inspect his work, Gandhiji was assassinated and the country was thrown into a chaos.

Each of my students taught me something new, particularly Subbarao. He made excellent use of Richard's *Geographical Factors in Indian History* to which I drew his attention long ago when it was published in the *Indian Antiquary*. He also had the courage to openly differ from me. And a particularly heated

discussion took place at Hyderabad on the question
of whether Series II tools should not be placed in
the Middle Palaeolithic or in a later period. I also
did not subscribe whole heartedly to his and Richard's
theory, according to which major cultures in India
had developed along the trans-continental routes. I
am quite sure that had he been alive, he would have
accepted the overwhelming evidence in favour of the
Middle Palaeolithic period as well as the political
and other reasons for the growth and development
of such cultures in India.

7

While Subbarao was left to devote his attention
to the Neolithic in south India, the small excavation at Nasik opened my eyes—my heart's desire—
to the period just before our recorded history. We
began under very auspicious circumstances. Had
Sali not given us the spouted pot and an unbroken
bowl from Jorwe on our trip to Nasik by bus, we
could not have immediately grasped the significance
of a single spout found below the weathered layer in
our small trench at Nasik. Nasik also helped me to
get a firm grip on pottery. This also happened by
chance. The preparation of the section on pottery
was left to Dr M.G. Dikshit but he joined the
Sagar University and so when I returned from
England after six months, I found that I had to begin
all over again. It was a painful but wholesome
experience.

Equally providential was our discovery of the
buried river channel of the Godavari filled with
many palaeoliths at Gangapur. Thus in one single
season I was instrumental in opening the gateway to
the prehistory and protohistory of Maharashtra,
thereby disproving the century-old view of the geologists and archaeologists that the Deccan was not
inhabited by Man as Gujarat and south India or
Sind and Punjab.

When Dr Karve and I were frequently going to
Langhnaj and Sabarmati, scholars as well as laymen
in Pune thought why we could not discover Stone
Age tools in Maharashtra? Why should we not pay
attention to Pune with its two ancient rivers? they
said. Dr Karve herself shared their views.

So after our third visit to Gujarat she and I, one
day, got into the Mula-Mutha, beyond the Bund
Garden and surveyed the river for a couple of hours.
When nothing but broken pieces of china and bones
and occasionally a few human skulls (because this
locality is the cremation and burial ground) came to
our lot, we were, out of measure, sad. Should we then
survey the river upstream? We wandered for several hours up and down the Vithal Wadi but with
little success. But luck again favoured me. One day
after my lecture on prehistory to the M.A. students
in sociology at the Deccan College, I told them how
the terraces could be best understood if we could go
over to the Mula-Mutha. For here, though we had
not found any tools, the remains of terraces were
clearly visible.

Thus we walked up to the Bund Garden and got
near the river. When I was explaining how the
thick red silt was formed, standing near the cliff on
the right bank, just below the Pumping Station, to
my great surprise, I saw the pebble conglomerate.
It was not so thick as we had seen on the Sabarmati.
However, I discovered within a few minutes a fine
olive green flake. While the flake was genuine, its
colour revealed in no uncertain way its age. It was
olive green, exactly like the tools from Gangapur,
near Nasik. A little later, I traced the remnants of
the ancient pebble bed covering the bedrock. After
this discovery we undertook a fresh survey of the
upper reaches of the Mutha and found excellent
evidence for the changes in the river-bed throughout
the Pleistocene epoch, the last epoch of the Cenozoic

Since then my eyes were always riveted on the terraces on either side of the Bund Garden. When after the Panshet flood the river overflowed its bank, I could visualise the scene of some ten to twenty thousand years ago, when for some reason not yet known, the river rose to a phenomenal height and a layer of black coloured silt lay all over the Koregaon Park and both sides of the Deccan College except the highest rock surface. During this great rise the diorite dyke which rises across my present residence (*Satchit-ananda*) up to the main college building— the present building of Linguistic Department—was high and dry and the place must have been the home of the Early Man for we (Shaikh and I) have found many tools—pebble tools as well as scrapers and cleavers in and around this dyke.

Hence, my colleagues say, half in joke and half seriously, if I were not still occupying the site of my prehistoric residence! No wonder, they say, that stone-tools gravitate towards me because I have been used to handling them all these ages! If one believes in the theory of *karma* and *vāsanā* as the propelling cause of the cycle of human existence—*saṁsāra*— then there is no reason why such observations should not carry a great deal of truth. Whether true or not, I have found these prehistoric studies of engrossing interest. And whenever I go to the countryside I find that nature talks to me about the ages gone by.

9

This excavation as well as the earlier one at Nasik had given me a very trusted lieutenant in Dr S.B. Deo. Though Deo was originally chosen for reconstructing the cultural history from Jain sources, chiefly in ardhamagadhi, he showed a keen aptitude for field-work. So after he had completed his thesis on the history of Jain monachism, he was gradually

absorbed in the Department and was given a permanent and decent appointment. A man of very
sparse habits and fewer wants, he would stand the
whole day in a trench and see that nothing — finds
nor layers — remains unobserved. With what great
care and devotion he would look after the pottery-
yard and maintain the daily record which would be
of great help to us in after-dinner sessions when we
would register the finds. How well he had imbibed
the training and spirit of the Deccan College may
be judged by the excellent work he did in Nepal and
Nagpur. The Deccan College is the only institution
in India which has kept pace with its programme of
excavation. Nor has it lagged behind in publishing
the results of the excavations.

Another trusted lieutenant I found in Shaikh—
Dr Z.D. Ansari. He had joined us as a photographer in 1945 having computed his probationary
period under J.P. Joglekar, one of the most experienced photographers in the Survey. Ever ready to
do any kind of work, Shaikh has shown exemplary
tenacity of purpose as well as character in achieving
what he set out to accomplish for himself as well as
for the Department. Hence it is no exaggeration to
say that whatever success I have achieved in establishing an archaeological department is due to the
selfless and devoted service of these two pupil-
assistants. When Deo was away in Nepal and then at
Nagpur, Shaikh was the one pillar on whom I could
always stand. It was their example which was emulated by others who came to me later.

10

From Nasik to Nevasa was a natural transition,
though I must say frankly that I had not heard of
Nevasa before. This time the invitation, or the
suggestion, came from the late Shri B.G. Kher, the
first Chief Minister of Bombay State. Kher was a
pious man besides being a scholar. He was interested
in Shri Jnanesvara, the Marathi saint-poet. Since

60 the saint had stayed for some time at Nevasa and composed the first commentary on the *Bhagavad Gītā* in a language other than Sanskrit, that is, Marathi, Kher thought that if an archaeologist dug at Nevasa he might find some objects belonging to Jnanesvaran and others of his time.

We went to Nevasa. Before we had gone to Nevasa, Dr Karve and I had explored several ancient sites on the banks of the Godavari and the Pravara. When we went we saw a huge mound, cut into two, some of its sides having been exposed by the local earth-grabbers. A huge section was thus open for anybody's inspection. Deo, my wife and I soon found that the mound was much older than Jnanesvara. Here one might dig up the whole of the past history of Western Maharashtra. And so we dug of which a full report has since been published.

But more than the archaeological history, what we and particularly my wife, were pleased to find was the interest the local people took in our work and the co-operation they gave us. This made our four seasons' stay memorable. Add to this the fact that the mound itself is an ideal camping ground encircled by clusters of *neem* trees. At the entrance of the mound stands the ancient temple, which is believed traditionally to be the seat of Jnanesvara where he had dictated the *Gītā* to Shri Satchidananda Baba.

Jnanesvara inspired all of us. First, was the discovery of stratified deposits of the Early Palaeolithic and the Middle Palaeolithic. Once when I was away at Pune, Shaikh and others had discovered a fine symmetrical chert flake from the Hathiwell locality during one of our Sunday explorations. This was shown to me when I returned. The flake was so unlike the early palaeolithic handaxes and cleavers and the later microliths and chalcedonic blade tools that I concluded that the flake must belong to the middle period of the Old Stone Age.

But not satisfied with this hasty conclusions, I felt that we should search for its proper location in the river cliff. In our search my wife also joined; she had still retained her interest in our work. And to the great joy of all of us Sarla discovered such a location right near our mound. The site was not far from the one where Shaikh had earlier discovered, a thin but well cemented gravel conglomerate with an animal fossil *in situ*.

Later, Shaikh discovered numerous fossils, some loose, but all belonging to the Middle or Upper Pleistocene. Even now when he goes to Nevasa, he does not fail to visit the river sections. For, we all hope one day he will discover a human fossil as well at Nevasa.

It was at Nevasa again that we discovered a few thick, long chalcedonic blades and burins. Unfortunately these were gathered from the surface. But they were so different from the hundreds of blades we found from the excavation that I had no option but to suggest that these were symptomatic of the Upper Palaeolithic which lay buried somewhere nearby.

After twenty years Dr Rajaguru told me that such a stratified deposit he and Dr Mujumdar had discovered, upstream of Inamgaon, on the Ghod river. Thus, Nevasa has turned out to be the first site in India where the three characteristic cultural manifestations of the Old Stone Age were clearly recognized. The excavations on the mound were no less significant. Careful digging under Deo and Shaikh and aided by my new pupils, Mate and Chapekar, and a German girl student, Valentina Rosen yielded positive results. For the first time we could obtain an idea of the houses of the Satavahana period, with their fine lime-surfaced floors. Just below the black earth we found the burials of an earlier age in earthen pots. Thus the first clue to Maharashtra's relations with the South in prehistoric

62   period (Karnataka and Tamil Nadu) was established.

It was this history of Man's continued development for more than 100,000 years that has been graphically displayed in our museum at the Deccan College. For enabling us to do so we shall be ever grateful to Shri B.G. Kher and Shri Jnanesvara.

11

The discovery at Nasik revived my dream of testing the truth of our Puranic legends. If Nasik could go back to 1000 B.C. and even earlier, could not the same be true of Maheshwar on the Narbada? I had read, while quite young, that here ruled King Sahasrarjuna of the Haihayas who alone among all other kings had defeated Ravana. Fortunately, Amrit Vasant Pandya and before him, Karandikar, had done some exploratory work at Maheshwar. While the objects discovered by Karandikar we had no opportunity to see, those discovered by Pandya I saw in the company of Dikshit at Vallabh Vidya Nagar. The rest of the story is well-known. But the point that I should like to stress here is the idea of a joint expedition and the support that I got from the three universities, particularly from the Maharaja Sayajirao University of Baroda. Dr Subbarao and his staff co-operated whole-heartedly. I was able to do here one of the richest Chalcolithic sites in India—one of the best jobs of my career. There is still some scope for more meaningful work as both Deo and I remind overselves whenever we meet.

At Maheshwar-Navadatoli the staff of the Maharaja Sayajirao University consisted of Dr R.N. Mehta, Dr S. Chaudhari, Ramesh Khatri and others —all Gujaratis. All of them not only became expert diggers but as brought a sense of mirth and hilarity to our camp. Maharashtrians are, as a rule, reserved. Not so the Gujaratis. After the day's work, and particularly on Saturday evenings, Chaudhari would invariably go for fishing, Mehta for swimming. After

dinner we would go boating. The boats there were 63
fairly big, all flat-bottomed and wide enough to
accommodate about forty persons. Thus our entire
camp could be accommodated. Then Chaudhari
would start singing which would give a fillip to the
hidden talents of Rasar for composing songs on our
work. Sutaria would sing devotional songs. On
holidays we arranged sports and competition. Some
of our workers including women also joined. There
was real comradarie. The three seasons' work at
Navdatoli have not only contributed an important
chapter to Indian archaeology but left an idelible
mark on the memory of all of us who had participated in it.

<h1>12</h1>

Maheshwar is an old site, having a magnificent
ghāta, a number of temples and memorials (*chhatris*)
built either at the instance of Rani Ahalyabai Holkar
of Indore or during her reign. Everyday while
going up and down the various localities—Mandal-
kho and others—I used to admire these beautiful
monuments. No doubt they were of recent period.
Should not these and similar monuments of the
18th-19th century find a place in our history of art
and architecture ? I, therefore, decided to photograph the Maheshwar monuments as well as the
century-old houses at Navdatoli. This foresight paid.

When I reached Pune I found a student who
had done history at the M.A. and could also
draw. When he asked me if he could do his Ph.D.
under my supervision I told him whether he would
be willing to work on the Maratha art and architecture. He and others—even scholars—wondered
whether the Marathas had anything to do with art,
busy as they always were in fighting and establishing
their hold wherever they went. The student asked
me if he could get reading material on this subject.
I told him that he would have to reconstruct the
entire history of Maratha art as nothing has been

written about it so far. He took up the challenge. *Maratha Architecture* appeared within a few years, and now we have a school of Mediaeval Archaeology flourishing under Dr M.S. Mate.

Another student, Pramod Gadre of Ahmadnagar College, prepared a thesis on the *Archaeology of Ahmadnagar* under my guidance. Unfortunately this splendid work has remained unpublished so far. This instance has been cited to illustrate that I am attracted by all aspects of archaeology—life in the past—not merely prehistory or protohistory.

13

In 1953, after my father's death, we happened to go to Nathadvara, one of the holiest places of Vaishnavas. While on the pilgrimage, I did not forget that it was the other end of the Aravallis, where the river Sabarmati originates and flows through North Gujarat. It was on its banks I had my baptism of prehistory. So the river Banas which flows by Nathadvara must have some traces of the Early Man. As luck would have it, one tool was found. And then I visualised the entire prehistory of Rajasthan. But who would reconstruct it?

Then I remembered that the late Dr D. N. Majumdar wanted to send a student for training and I had advised him to send him after he had completed his M.A. So when Misra came, I asked him whether he would explore Rajasthan. With what success Misra discharged the trust placed in him is well-known. His explorations in the Berach, the Banas and the Luni were followed by excavations at Bagor and Tilwara. Having gathered this experience he is now digging at Bhimbetaka in Madhya Pradesh with conspicuous success.

I particularly welcomed Misra, because I had realised that archaeology—particularly prehistory—should be firmly based on anthropology. It is not

enough to discover objects. These have to be inter-   **65**
preted—an exercise that requires an insight into
the life of the primitives, their customs, manners, and
social structure. While I myself could do little with
all the duties I was saddled with, I had always
thought that well-trained students in social anthropology would be an asset to the Department.

An edge to this line of thinking was given when
at Ahar, near Udaipur, I found that the houses of
the Bhils who still live at the foot of the Dhūlkota
mound, were modelled exactly on the 4000 year-old
houses we had discovered in our excavation. Who
were the ancestors of the Ahar or those of the
Navdatoli culture? If they were aboriginals, as one
school of thought maintained that they were, there
should be some traces of similarity in the life style
of the present Bhils whose material remains we had
excavated.

Five

Understanding Archaeology

1. *Ethno-Archaeology, Epigraphy, and Palaeography*
2. *Archaeological Chemistry* 3. *Tekkalkota and Neolithic Culture* 4. *The Upper Palaeolithic Culture* 5. *In Search of the Aryans, B.B. Lal and Hastinapur Episode* 6. *Inamgaon, Dr. Dhavalikar, Bio-Archaeology.*

YET another student from the Anthropological Department of Lucknow university was entrusted with the study of ethno-archaeology. Since ethno-archaeology is not a particular problem of Ahar only, but of all proto-historic cultures in India, its study was made a permanent feature of the Archaeology Department of the Deccan College with the appointment of Dr Malati Nagar.

Except for the temporary appointment of a lecturer in Ancient Indian Culture and a lecturer in Environmental Archaeology, after Zeuner's visit to India and his close association with the work at the Deccan College, no planned development of the department was possible until 1958-59, when the University Grants Commission decided to start a Department of Ancient Indian History and Archaeology in six universities.

I took this opportunity to create a lecturership in Epigraphy and Palaeography because these subjects were utterly neglected in India. There was another

reason as well. Discussions with Richards in London
had stimulated my interest in places and persons in
history. And I was convinced that not only are the
former significant in India or, for that matter, anywhere in the world but also the latter, particularly
in India and perhaps also in South-east Asia. I found
that both these offered stratigraphical and chronol-
ogical information to chart out the growth and development of man's culture from age to age, more
than any other facts.

I was so much fascinated by this material—viz.
place and personal names that I found in Gujarat
inscriptions became the main theme of my lecture in
1944 that I delivered at the Bombay University for
the Thakkar Vassonji Lectures, though I could, if I
had so wished, lecture on the prehistory of Gujarat
on which I had then done some research.

However, my lecture was the first full-fledged
and systematic study of place names in India. Small
and large administrative units have been reconstruct-
ed on the basis of these names which gave an excellent idea of the way how our political units worked
in our country. Two basic requirements for this
study may here be mentioned. First, the student
should belong to the same region that he has taken
up for study so that he or she can have a better
knowledge of the persons and places of the region
than his teacher. Secondly, some knowledge of
Sanskrit is essential as also knowledge of the language in which the inscriptions are written.

Unfortunately, this kind of work which I consider to be the unique contribution of the Deccan
College to the study of historical geography and
cultural ethnography of India is little known. But
when the history of such studies will be written,
the true value of the contribution of the Deccan
College will be appreciated. Not satisfied with
what I did, I thought of depicting the ancient geography of Gujarat and Maharashtra and some parts

of Karnataka on the walls in the new building of our College. When a savant of historical geography saw our mural depiction he remarked, "We did not have the opportunity to do anything of this kind because we never got devoted students who could do such a thing".

I should also like to mention that the discovery of new inscriptions and copper plates by Dr Shobhana Gokhale of the University Department was made possible because provision was made for teaching and field-research in this subject at the Deccan College and in the Pune University. Whether there are students or not, if our past history is to be fully resuscitated then provision must be made for such studies in at least two or more universities in this country. For several reasons the epigraphical branch of the Survey cannot cope with new discoveries as well as the vast material that have already been collected for more than a century.

Further, when the opportunity came, besides making provision for epigraphy and palaeography, I also set up a chemical laboratory with an archaeological chemist to man it to strengthen the studies of these two subjects.

2

The results were soon apparent. The gap between the early historic and the chalcolithic habitation which I had discovered at Nevasa on the basis of the thick layer of black soil was first confirmed by Professor Zeuner, and later proved by scientific tests conducted by Dr G. G. Majumdar. Mujumdar's chemical analysis or the entire 25 feet profile by taking samples at intervals of 6 inches showed that the humic content was more or less similar on the top soil (that is, in the present black soil layer), in the intervening black soil layer, and in the layer which is at the very bottom above the yellowish silt. How he later confirmed his conclusions by examin-

ing several samples at different sites in the Deccan
Trap is known to those who keep track of archaeological developments in this country. Equally
known is his imitation of the megalithic Black-and-
Red ware and Painted Grey Ware.

Another colleague of Mujumdar, Dr S.N. Rajaguru, has thrown more positive light on the climatic
conditions during the Pleistocene by his study of the
river gravels in Maharashtra. To these studies our
pupils, particularly Statira Guzdar, had contributed
a great deal. Her thesis was adjudged best by Dr
Butzer who is an international expert on palaeocli-
matic studies and archaeology. All these were
possible due to the interdiciplinary studies that we
could undertake at the Deccan College. Now with
the addition of a palaeobotanist (M.D. Kajale), a
palaeontologist (Dr G.L. Badam), and an ethno-
archaeologist (Dr Malati Nagar), it is hoped to cover
as many facets of the ever-widening horizon of
archaeolgy as possible. The Maharashtra Government also upgraded the existing lecturerships in
ancient Indian culture, art and architecture as well
as environmental archaeology and field-archaeology
and museums though, unfortunately, these posts have
not been made permanent. Side by side with these
developments, new areas in India are being explored and steps are being taken to fill up the lacuna
in our knowledge of the Stone Ages or later proto-
historic cultures. However, I must say that it is
certainly unfortunate that students from distant
regions like Orissa, Uttar Pradesh, and Andhra
Pradesh have not found opportunities to continue
the work for which they were trained. The reason
is simple. Institutions like the Deccan College are
few. In other universities the teachers are saddled
with so much teaching work that they hardly get
any time for going to the field. And it is worse
when the callous Head of the Department does not
allow his assistants to publish their work they have
done for years on end. Naturally, there is acute
frustration among research students. These students

naturally think of the opportunities which the students find the Deccan College for their research and envy those who have found a permanent footing here.

3

As I said, my research of the Neolithic culture in Andhra-Karnataka belt was cut short because of Gandhiji's assassination. So when a student from this region, M.S. Nagaraja Rao, came to work under me for his Ph. D., I welcomed him and with his help we first excavated Tekkalkota and later Sangankallu in Bellary district. Indeed, I was so much fascinated by the former site that I invited all the members of the Department to participate in intensive and extensive excavations at Tekkalkota. I always feel that newly acquired knowledge should be shared and opportunities must be found to disseminate it. A significant contribution to this subject was made by Paddayya's trial dig at Kodikal in Shorapur Doab. Here he has also uncovered a camp site of the Early Man at Hunsgi. Thus I can reasonably hope that the Neolithic problem, which was left at an interesting stage at Tekkalkota, will be pursued with vigour. While there are, and must be, many sites like Tekkalkota, Terrace I at Tekkalkota, is so large that if excavated for two reasons, it will afford a good insight into the settlement pattern of the Neolithic people.

As expected, Dr Nagaraja Rao's excavations at Tekkalkota and subsequent excavations conducted by us at Sangankallu not only gave us the picture of the settlement pattern of the Neolithic people but at the latter site we also uncovered two more earlier periods in the Stone Age—Mesolithic and pre-Mesolithic.

Now, one more link remained to explore, namely the Upper Palaeolithic. With its discovery we will have the entire prehistoric cultural chain reconstruc-

ted right from the early Stone Age down to the
historic period through the Neolithic and Megalithic
so far as South India is concerned.

4

The Upper Palaeolithic culture came to be discovered by a persistent and methodological enquiry.
While exploring around Renigunta in Andhra
Pradesh besides finding handaxes and cleavers of the
Early Stone Age and points and scrapers of chert,
etc. of the Middle Palaeolithic, Murty had also
discovered a few typical blades and burins in green-
ish quartzite. When I saw these I was immediately struck by their unique character. They were
quite large and thick, typically Upper Palaeolithic,
and almost identical to those I had got in exchage
from Musée de L'Homme in Paris. And, I rightly
argued, that there must be more in that area consti-
tuting a distinct cultural niche. Repeated searches
yielded more than 600 artifacts and also in the adjoining district of Cuddappa at Yerragondapallam and
elsewhere Reddy discovered a large number of
such objects.

Then I remembered that at Kurnool in the Billa
Surgam caves, Bruce Foote and his son had found
bone tools like those of Megdalenian of France. So
Murty was advised to dig there. It is indeed a
difficult forest terrain to forage about without any
trace of human habitation. But his effort was well-
rewarded. The excavation of the cave yielded typical Upper Palaeolithic bone tools.

Thus by constant thinking and planning, by
giving opportunities to our young teachers and students, the missing links in our history and prehistory
are being gradually filled up. That is how Murty's
discoveries in Chittoor and Kurnool districts were
confirmed by Sali when following his surface explorations at Patne in Dhulia district, he dug for the
Deccan College. and found excellent evidence

regarding the Middle, Upper Palaeolithic and the Mesolithic cultures in several trenches.

Whether it be archaeology or crime detection, a clue has to be scientifically and methodically pursued and wherever this healthy principle is persued success follows. In these particular cases, two very complex questions were involved, namely the postulation of two cultural stages spanning no less than 1,00,000 of years implying slow but steady progress made by man not only in India but also in Europe and Western Asia.

Of course, when I first postulated the existence of the Middle Palaeolithic my assumption was opposed by Subba Rao at Hyderabad in 1958, as I have already mentioned. The same happened in 1972 when Dr R. V. Joshi, one of my very first students, like Subba Rao, with his wide experience thought that it was still premature to talk of the existence of a true Upper Palaeolithic cultural state even though I showed him the Upper Palaeolithic sites at Renigunta. Joshi and others have now accepted my thesis.

I, of course, did not rest satisfied with this willing or unwilling acceptance. A theory or a model, when formulated before or after some ground-work, has to be scientifically proved and tested. This is certainly difficult in archaeology, particularly in India, as I have pointed out in the D. N. Majumdar Lectures. Be that as it may, one has to be aware of it and take steps accordingly to understand the process. It was in this spirit that we embarked upon horizontal excavations at Navdatoli in 1957-59, at Nevasa in 1959-61, at Ahar in 1961-62, and at Inamgaon in 1968 and later at Tekkalkota and Sangankallu.

At Navdatoli the problem of the Iranian contact or influence intrigued me which was indicated by the spout of channel and stems of goblets as well as a few characteristic designs that I came across. While extensive excavations have given us good idea of the life of the inhabitants some 3,500 years ago still we do not know who they were. There is not a day when I do not wonder what these people were doing with so many goblets in their small, one-room tenaments when they had nothing but stone chips to light their daily fire. Or were these kept perpetually burning once these were lighted?

It is now more than fifteen years that these problems have been broached. Neither we nor the local scholars who now wish to keep outsiders away from sharing their knowledge have taken any steps to understand these problems. The first step is to find out whether the goblets were confined only to Navdatoli or were fairly well distributed in Malwa or Western Madhya Pradesh. A village-to-village survey, particularly where there are ancient mounds, can easily solve this problem. One day some of these sites will have to be excavated, as we did at Navdatoli.

When I was on way to Maheshwar, or a little earlier, I met V. S. Wakankar of Ujjain in the Prince of Wales Museum. Learning about my interest he not only willingly joined our excavations, but spread before me his collections of potsherds from a number of sites in Malwa. Thus I was convinced that we were not digging a solitary site, but a site which might represent the culture of Malwa or Western Madhya Pradesh. During these twenty-five years I have been telling him about the unique kind of cups or goblets that had so far not been found anywhere else in Malwa.

Dr Wakankar who has gained considerable experience by study, training, and continuous travel in Malwa and elsewhere told me recently that such cups having a base and a stem seemed to be confined only to Nemad (South Malwa) as these could not be found anywhere else—at Ujjain, Mandasore, Vidisha,

74   and Eran. Thus my initial response and later study seem to be finding confirmation. My final view is that these goblets must have been brought by the rich people from Western Asia possibly across the Arabian Sea and then taken up the Narmada. In this way my original suggestion that some Iranian influence was at work at Maheshwar-Navdatoli would find some confirmation. What is needed therefore is an intensive exploration of south Malwa.

The excavations at Ahar (1961-62), Dwarka (1964), and Tripuri were all chiefly undertaken to solve, if possible, the Aryan problem, and to understand the related problem—the truth or otherwise of the accounts given in the epics and Puranas. For giving me an opportunity to probe these problems, I am thankful to Dr Srivastava, the then Director of Archaeology of Rajasthan, Shri J.M. Nanavati Director of Archaeology of Gujarat and Shri, Jayantilal Thakur and Dr D.P. Mishra, the then Chief Minister of Madhya Pradesh. The Deccan College could not have thought of undertaking excavations at Ahar, near Udaipur in southern Rajasthan. But I think I was destined to throw some positive light on this much neglected area, and particularly its contribution to our knowledge of the Copper technology.

5

Since Lal's discovery at Hastinapur in 1952-53 I have been anxious, like others. to know more about the Aryans, B.B. Lal had said that the Painted Grey Ware Culture goes back to the Early Aryans. Though I did not agree with this conclusion and I had always maintained that the Painted Grey Ware culture could not have belonged to the *Mahābhārata* period, if our tradition is any guide. You may date the *Mahābhārata* period as you please but its age certainly begins at the end of the entire period begining with the Aryans or the Puranic dynasties.

In one of the lectures that I delivered at the Tata Staff Club at Pune where Professor R.D. Choksey, one of the Directors was in the chair, I pointed out after giving an account of the excavation at Navdatoli the possibility of the Navadatolians being a branch of the Aryans, because of the similarity of its pottery with that of the Iranians. I had also impressed upon my audience the necessity of extensive excavations at Hastinapur to prove (or disprove) the theory of Lal. After the lecture, Prof. Choksey told me that if funds were the only problem then he could help. To my great surprise and joy, the two Tata Trusts promised to give Rs. 20,000 each for a period of three seasons.

I always thought that given our modest requirements, unlike those of the Archaeological Survey of India which camp out like the splendid Mughals, the money that the Tatas promised should be enough for a fairly reliable horizontal-cum-vertical dig. Now, of course, with prices spiralling at least double that amount of money would be required. However when funds were made available I discussed with the then Director General of Archaeology in India of my plan of digging at Hastinapur. The director drew my attention to the convention that a site once dug by X should not be allowed to be dug by Y. This monopolistic attitude of the government has come in the way of our knowledge of the Painted Grey Ware. More than twenty years have gone by since then and the Survey has done nothing about Hastinapur. In a recent symposium on the *Rāmāyana* and *Mahābhārata* at Bhopal, Prof. Lal himself said that what he had dug at Hastinapur was indeed very little. If it were so, as indeed it is, can we still continue to go on holding such an important hypothesis ?

Anyway the Director General said that I could select any other Painted Grey Ware site I liked but not Hastinapur. He was kind enough to place a jeep and an assistant at our Disposal who had worked

76   with him in the exploration of the Painted Grey
Ware sites. For about two weeks the late Dr Subba
Rao and I examined several sites in the Saraswati
Valley in the erstwhile Bikaner State. But we could
not come by a large and promising site to repay an
excavation which could shed light on the Painted
Grey Ware culture. Thus an excellent opportunity
was lost on account of the rigid attitude of the
Archaeological Survey of India.

It was this inflexible attitude which again stood
in my way of conducting excavations at Lucknow
in 1975. The incident is worth relating. Lucknow is
supposed to be the ancient Lakshmanapur or Laksh-
manavati, its founder being no other than Lakshman,
the brother of Rama. So, while I was there for
delivering the late Dr D.N. Majumdar Lecture local
scholars and some university professors suggested
that the Deccan college should excavate at Lucknow
to acquaint them with the antiquity of their city.
I told them that it should be excavated by U.P.
archaeologists, but they were keen that we should
undertake this excavation. I asked them to arrange
for funds and to my great surprise this was done in
a day or so.

But when the Deccan College approached the
Director of Archaeology in India we were told that
the site was to be dug by Prof. B.B. Lal and his
operation Rāmāyaṇa is already afoot. I may say our
work would have furthered the objectives of Lal's
plan, and not hindered it. Furthermore some money
and time could have been saved. Unfortunately,
as it so happened, he could not dig at Ayodhya for
reason best known to him. And this site which
would have required at least three seasons of unre-
mitting work, if not more, remains still undug.

Meanwhile, the citizens of Lucknow lost an
opportunity to know the age of their city. The loss
is not ours, of the Deccan College, but of the
Archaeological Department. Why? Had the Stan-

ding Committee given us permission to excavate one of the members would have lost his monopoly over some parts of U.P. Thus, the ghosts of Nawā-bashāhī are still dogging us. I am reminded of a similar incident which Dr Wheeler told me soon after he came to India. One of his newly appointed officers did not want the Deccan College to carry out explorations in the Bellary district. Wheeler said: "My boy, there is work for 500 persons. So you go ahead!" Unfortunately, this wholesome advice was forgotten soon after he left India. The Archaeological Department thinks in regional terms but cultural problems transcend regional boundaries !

To revert to Rajasthan. After visiting Jaipur and Jodhpur, Subba Rao and I reached Udaipur. Here when I saw the huge mound, called Dhulkot, on the outskirts of the city, I was curious to know the part the site had played in the cultural development of Rajasthan and its neighbours, that is to say, Gujarat in the south and Madhya Pradesh in the east. Already R. C. Agarwala, an officer of the Rajasthan Department of Archaeology, had carried out preliminary excavations which yielded pottery known today as the Black-and-Red Ware of Ahar. Similar pottery had been found in the lowest layers of Navdatoli.

So, with the Tata funds and cooperation of the Rajasthan Government, we dug at Ahar. And it proved that its local name—Tambavati (Copper City)—was based on the fact that some 4,000 years ago, its inhabitants smelted copper from local ore and made axes and other copper implements. Had we continued, we would have certainly learnt much more about this Copper Age city. But we were politely told that this work could be left to the local scholars to accomplish. It is now 15 years since we had left Ahar and nothing has been done. The local scholars are still to be born!

Our excavations at Dwarka and Tripuri not only

helped me to understand something about the antiquity of the Puranic sites, but also explained why our epics and the Puranas grew thicker and thicker as a result of interpolations and when. Though there is considerable scope for more work at both these sites, it will not be wrong if I say that the actual truth about their antiquity remains still unknown.

Dr Jayantilal Thakkar and Dr Dwarka Prasad Mishra felt, and possibly feel even now, that Dwarka and Tripuri are thousands of years old and go back to the times of Shri Krishna and Tarakasura. However I am of the opinion that their story could not be taken back beyond the first century B.C. in case of the former and sixth century B.C. in case of the latter.

At Tripuri, I thought of a new experiment which I should like to call "Archaeological Federation." I sent out invitation to the M. S. University of Baroda and the University of Sagar to take part in my experiment. Instead of all the three teams working at one site under the super vision of one Director, each team was advised to complete the excavation of one site within a specified time. The report of each site was to be prepared separately and could also be published separately, if so desired.

This arrangement, I thought, would give sufficient incentive to each participating institution in the excavation work which originally was to last for several years, because Dr Mishra had placed a large amount of money at my disposal. Unfortunately, none of the sections that the three institutions dug yielded any clue of the prehistoric phase, as at Maheswar and Navdatoli. And since I was primarily interested in this problem, the M. S. University and the Deccan College withdrew, allowing the Sagar University to continue the excavations, if it so desired. So far they have dug for three seasons, but have not found anything prehistoric.

These excavations have convinced me that the
only way so introduce some realism into our epic
and Puranic studies and beliefs is by evcavating the
sites mentioned in the epics and Purāṇas. Unfortunately, there is no institution in Madhya Pradesh which
can tackle this problem. If outsiders are prevented
from solving this interesting and important problem
which touches the heart of our cultural development
then the problem will ever remain unsolved. Hence
any attempt to keep out others seems meaningless.
It is forgotten that the divisions of the country in the
past and at present were and are made for administrative convenience only. Past cultural processes
which now archaeology and anthropology unravel
know no geographical barriers. Hence the dog in
the manger policy will be suicidal. In fact, the
need of the hour, in a developing country like India,
is for greater cooperation and collaboration between
institutions not only within a town but within
different states as well. Archaeological studies are
becoming multi-disciplinary and no single institution or state has the resources or the expertise at
its disposal.

The intensive study of the Navdatoli lithic blade
industry led me to make a few hypotheses about the
socio-economic condition of the ancient Navdato-
lians. How far are these true? These models, or
still better hypotheses, have to be proved by careful
excavations at Navdatoli. Failing, the observations
can also be checked at other sites like Navdatoli. I
was on the lookout for one such site in Maharashtra.
Nevasa did not offer good scope, for the site was
found disturbed by the later occupants.

6

What I was so anxiously looking for was offered
by Inamgaon—a completely undisturbed site on the
bank of the Ghod river not too far from Pune. At
Inamgaon, I was anxious to know the unit of the
family. This could have been fairly easily known

at Navdatoli had we kept a strict note of all the potshreds, particularly the number of the channel spouts, the stems of the goblets and the necks of the vessels found in each oval or square house. Unfortunately, we were not seized of such larger questions at that time. We were still in that general "pottery phase" as taught by Wheeler and expounded by Sir Leonard Woolley. In fact, a question of this kind has ever been asked anywhere in India or anywhere else except in the very recent excavations of American Indian sites in the U.S.A.

Soon after I landed in London when I met Codrington he drew my attention to his article in *Indian Antiquary* on the cultural study of Ajanta paintings. It was a brief but quite a novel attempt to understand the precise nature of the material aspects of Indian culture.

When I Joind the Deccan College, a monograph on the Nagarjunakonda sculptures had just been published by Longhurst. I showed that to Naik, and asked him if he would like to undertake a similar study. To my surprise and joy, he analysed the entire monograph and all the sculptures mentioned therein and this was published in the *Bulletin* of the Deccan College. It is a much better and more scientifie study than the similar study done on the Amaravati sculptures. But Naik not being as good an artist as Sivaramamurti, the quality of the various reproduction in his book is not good.

Later, when Dhavalikar came, he undertook a study of Sanchi and Ajanta. The latter study is well done because during that period a number of excavations had been undertaken. We now know the precise time-range of a number of objects. Add to this the maturity of the scholar. Along with Shaikh, Dhavalikar has also shown great proficiency in excavating the remains of the mud-built houses at Inamgaon. He has kept himself abreast of the current developments abroad in archaeology and has also attempted

In understanding the settlement pattern during Chalcolithic times. This is not only a new, but a desira-
ble, study of our past cultures. It is on these lines
that future excavations in India have to proceed instead of the current hit-and-run methods of digging.

Because Ansari (Shaikh), Dhavalikar, Rasar, and
Padwal are working continuously at Inamgoan all
of them have developed such expertise and skill,
like a doctor or a surgeon, in detecting the existence
and then exposing the remains of the round, square
or rectangular mud houses. It is difficult to find their
equals anywhere in India.

A few American students having participated in
this prehistoric house excavation have now planned
a small excavation of their own near Inamgaon. We
have further tried to ascertain the habit of each
family from the study of animal bones found in each
of the houses. Such bio-archaeological questions have
been recently asked by the archaeologists in Europe
and elsewhere. All developing disciplines must ask
new questions but such questions can be asked only
after some ground-work. Unfortunately suggestions
of this type will remain only on paper, because a
majority of our excavations are still confined to a
few trenches and recovery of finds and personal
supervisions are absent. Unless there is day-to-day
discussion both in the field and in the evening, which
the Americans call "feed-back", mere formulations
of models and theories are of little use. Side by side
there should be a multi-disciplinary approach. This
is as a rule shunned, and secrecy is the rule among
the scholars. Unless things change archaeology in
India has no future and mine would remain only a
cry in the wilderness.

Nehru Fellowship

1. *Nehru Fellowship* 2. *Miracle in Kashmir* 3. *On archaeological excavations* 4. *Mainly Personal* 5. *Rare Hospitality* 6. *Scientific Study of Astrology* 7. *Awards* 8. *Attitude to God.*

BY 1968, I had gained a fairly good idea of the Stone Age and other cultures, practically of all India. What remained was a first-hand acquaintance with the sites in Kashmir, Kanyakumari, Dwarka, and Bhubhaneshwar so that a more integrated picture of the cultural development of India could be had. Though I was aware of the gaps in my knowledge of Indian prehistory, frankly speaking, I had not thought of filling these gaps. I was preoccupied with my first love, the archaeological interpretation of the *Rāmāyaṇa* and *Purāṇas*. Then suddenly an opportunity came. One evening in 1967-68 a letter reached me at Pune redirected from Baroda. It said that my name had been recommended by the Gujarat University for Nehru Fellowsip, and that I should send my bio-data and the details of the subject I should like to work on to be forwarded to the Jawaharlal Nehru Memorial Committee. At first, I could not understand what this fellowship meant, for only on the previous day, I had read in the papers about Nehru scholarships and had thought of recommending the name of one of my students for a scholarship. I thought if I should apply for a fellowship at all! But when all the particulars of

Though Nehru Fellowship was awarded to me when I was on the wrong side of sixty, it gave me an unique opportunity to visit distant prehistoric sites in India. Not only was I able to see the sites on the south-eastern coast around Madras, but I also saw many sites at Kanyakumari and Rameswaram. As a result of the inspection of the century-old sites I could offer a different interpretation of the so-called *teris* (fossil) sand dunes. A visit to Garo Hills in Assam (now in Arunachal Pradesh) also helped me to establish the existence of the Early Stone Age culture in that region which the scholars refused to accept because they had always thought that Assam could never have the Early Stone Age Culture on account of ecological (climatic) and other reasons. Later, while studying the geo-morphology of the region, I found that this region was at one time one landmass and the Bay of Bengal took shape subsequently and, hence, in spite of marked climatic difference, the Early Man must have migrated to the Garo Hills from India proper as also his successors — the Middle Palaeolithic and even the Meso-lithic people. Assam's contact with south-east Asia is, at present, well documented.

2

I had planned to go to Kashmir also just to acquaint myself with the true glacial deposits but not with a view to making any discovery there. This could not be even dreamt of because when De Terra, Paterson and Wadia before them had spent months and years and they could not find any evidence of the existence of the Early Man, how could I ? But miracle does happen and it happened. Along with R.K. Pant and Sardarilal of the Archae-ological Survey of India in Srinagar, I was examin-ing the glacial deposits on the Liddar mentioned by De Terra and Paterson. As I had never seen an Ice

Age glacial conglomerate, though I had seen hundreds of ordinary river conglomerates in Gujarat, Maharashtra, Andhra, Karnataka. Madhya Pradesh, Uttar Pradesh, and Tamil Nadu, I was examining piece by piece each clod of earth and lump of stone as they came out. One curious-looking stone I kept as a child would keep a fine glossy pebble found on a river bank or a sea shore. It definitely showed some ice action. Lo! and behold, the next moment, my eyes fell upon the wavy edge of a large broken greyish stone. The rest of the stone was inside the section, so we were not sure whether it was a tool—a man-made thing or just a broken piece of stone. Not expecting any tool, I took it out though normally we photograh the object before its removal. To my great joy and surprise the flake bore all the signs of a man-made tool !

Particularly striking was the protuberance, called "bulb of percussion" in our jargon. So, here was the first evidence of the existence of the Early Man in Kashmir valley during the First Ice Age or soon after. My colleagues were indeed surprised and glad that such a thing had been discovered in their state. And then they remarked : "Never had any prehistorian examined so carefully, so-called boulder conglomerate. A large party, under a very experienced and well-known Indian prehistorian had come to this site but after looking at this deposit cursorily they went sight seeing." Later we found a hand-axe too at the same spot in a layer just above the boulder conglomerate. This time we took all the normal precautions and photographed the tool before it was extracted.

This was indeed an epoch-making discovery. Many scholars in India and abroad were glad when they heard of the discovery. Some even congratulated me. Some were, however, jealous, and went to the length of saying that it was all propaganda. Luckily before the campaign was started, I had published an article giving full details and illustra-

Not content with this runaway success, I also organised a joint expedition with the Archaeological Survey which consisted of highly experienced geologists and prehistorians. We examined this section at Pahlgam and many other sites in Kashmir. This was followed by one more search, but this time I was not one of the party. The results of these two explorations in Kashmir were later published in *World Archaeology*. Thus any lurking doubt about the existence of the Early Man in the Ice Age Kashmir has now been removed once for all.

3

The Kashmir episode has been related in some detail, because I always believed that any new discovery in archaeology, if it is really to be sustained, should be tested by repeated observations and excavations, preferably by different scholars. That is why Langhnaj was first excavated by me (thrice), then independently by Subba Rao, and finally by Dr Kennedy and Dr Corvinus. No scholar, however great or known for his skill of observation, should claim omniscience. It was because of this reason that I wanted to dig at Hastinapur and had secured enough funds as well. But the authorities thought otherwise. It is now nearly twenty-five years since this site was first excavated but, alas, we are today no wiser than what we were in 1953.

After my discoveries in Kashmir, I felt that it was necessary to strengthen the prehistory branch of our Department by appointing a specialist who should not only be a geologist and a prehistorian, but who should have experience of glacial or ice-bound regions, so that the Deccan College can undertake such studies when the opportunity came. Fortunately the UGC, under the Special Assistance Scheme to Universities, gave a Professor in prehistory and lecturer each in paleotology, palaeobotany, and ethno-archaeology. So with the addition of this staff, the Deccan College is now the only institution in India which is equipped to make use of multidimensional approaches to the understanding of our past cultures.

Let me give another example of the narrow and selfish attitude of a scholar. We wanted to ascertain the truth of the so-called Oldwwai Industry at Mahadeo Piparia on the Narmada. Unfortunately, the discoverer had not the courage to show us the exact spot on the section which he thought was the oldest deposit on the Narmada. The discoverer forgot that truth will be out sooner or later and that he could not hide it for long. The Piltdown forgery could not remain a secret, once the scientists had found ways of distinguishing between the old and young bones. If any discipline or science expects complete honesty from its devotee, it is certainly archaeology. Very often, the discovery in archaeology, big or small, important or unimportant, is made by a single man and therefore he must give an honest account of his discovery. But there are scholars who do not give out the full truth.

The picture of India that thus emerged or stood before me as a result of personal inspection of the sites in the distant corners as well as in the heart of India, such as in the forest of Dang, was that in spite of great and marked climatic and geological contrasts as well as ecological variations, the Early Man and his successors, had manufactured or were inspired to manufacture almost identical tools. This identity of material culture is indeed surprising. It may be asked why. I am of the opinion that in spite of ecological differences and probably ethnic differences as well (of which we have no idea at present) homogeneity of material culture which is to be found in all the three continents can be explained on the assumption of the minimal needs.

It was, also destined that I should devote the maximum time of my daily life to archaeology. During my school and college days, though I did attend to some household work, generally my parents spared me from attending social functions. As a result I was left to myself. Even when I settled down in Pune I led a life of a recluse. In the first place, we lived far away from the city, and it was not so easy to go to the city from the Deccan College for want of transport facilities. My wife too was of the same temperament as I. She loves solitude and, hence, avoids all social contact. The influence of such saints as Shri Upasani Maharaj of Sakori, Shri Aurobindo and the Mother and Shri Raman Maharshi had developed in her an other-worldly attitude. Thus our life developed on a line which is not quite common.

Though both of us disliked social life and kept ourselves away from enjoying the normal married life, both of us enjoyed roaming in the hills, forests and river banks, and could do without the many necessities of life. When we went to Kasmir, soon after marriage, we cooked our own food and instead of shopping filled our eyes with the beauties of nature. After joining the Deccan College, the ancient monuments in Andhra, Karnataka and Tamil Nadu were visited in the same manner camping like a gipsy family wherever we went. Thus my wife could, and did, accompany me in many archaeological excavations. When I fell ill on the Sabarmati, my wife immediately joined me and was with me till the end of the expedition.

In the 1945-46 expedition she extricated us from a very peculiar and difficult predicament. In those days, and perhaps even now, there were no hotels or rest-houses in out-of-the-way-places like Valasna on the bank of the Sabarmati in North Gujarat. For staying at such places one had to depend upon the hospitality of the headman of the village. Valasna at that time was under a semi-independent chief, owing allegiance to the Gaikwad of Baroda. We had planned to survey the upper reaches of the Sabarmati and selected Valasna for our stay as it was right on the river bank. With a letter of introduction from the *vahivtdar* (collector of Mehsua) we reached Valasna with our fairly large camp, including two Gurkha policemen. Looking at our clothes, our equipments, and particularly two women, my wife and Dr Karve, the local people including the school children thought that a cinema company or a circus party had invaded their village.

Scarcely had I expected that the news would have reached the Thakur Saheb (the village headman), when I sought an interview with him. To our great surprise and dismay, not only did Thakur Saheb refuse to receive me, but ordered us to leave his village immediately, bag and baggage, in a truck that he was willing to offer. The bus that had brought us had gone and no other conveyance would be available for another twenty-four hours!

Then my wife sought an interview with Rani Saheb, and taking with her the letter of introduction she met Thakur Saheb, and convinced both of them that we were all respectable people and that we did not belong to a circus party but to the university. Later, he became our friend and the next year he relished the fish and flesh that we had brought when Professor Zeuner paid a visit to Gujarat.

In 1953-54 when we excavated at Maheshwar and Navdatoli on the Narmada, my wife had accompanied us and remained with us throughout the entire season. This is one of the most beautiful stretches of the Narmada with a broad expanse and a fine *ghāta* and a towering temple of Śiva inside the old Muslim fort built by Rani Ahalyabai. Besides there are several small old and new temples. On the opposite side, at Navdatoli, there are a number of prehistoric mounds, still strewn with 3000-year old relics, potsherds, microliths and occasional beads of semi-precious stones and possibly coins of the early historic period.

Since my wife loved solitude and enjoyed roaming from place to place and collecting antiquities she would everyday either cross the Narmada and visit this temple or that or go alone from one mound to another. During one of her visits, she collected numerous beads from Mound IV at Navdatoli. Hence she concluded that there must have been a bead factory on that mound. Since we were busy excavating other mounds, we did not pay much attention to this discovery. But in 1957 when I went to Maheshwar once again, I recalled her discovery and suggested the excavation of the Mound VI to Dr N.R. Banerji, the then Superintendent of Excavation. But he thought that since the Deccan College had already conducted an earlier excavation, we should undertake this excavation also. With what wonderful results—houses and beautiful pottery, some still intact—we excavated from this mound is well known. We spent two long seasons here and would like to be there again.

Likewise Nevasa turned out to be a very rich mine though not a Pandora's Box, as an English friend, unwittingly and mistakenly described it in his *Review* of our *report*. We had encamped right on the mound, overlooking the river, and close by the Jnanesvar Temple. This was another beautiful site. a short distance from the present town and, hence, a fairly clean mound.

My wife also joined our river surveys in search of the palaeoliths, as she was now fairly well experienced. In one of these surveys, she helped us discover a section with Series II tools, now placed in the Middle Palaeolithic, because of stratigraphical reason. However, there were occasions when because of ill-health or other reasons, she could not accompany me on our expeditions. On such occasions she stayed alone in the large and solitary Bungalow No. 3 at the Deccan College or later in our own house. It would certainly be very trying for a person to live like this for days and months, when not quite well, and so far removed, even at the Deccan College, from other friends. However, she bore these interludes with courage and fortitude. Even at home, I was not much of a company because right from 4 a.m. till evening, I would be reading or writing. Finding me so much engrossed in my work, sitting alone and thinking, she would often remark, "You have married the Muse of Archaeology and not me!" However, she would be reconciled to her lot. I must say that but for my wife's constant care and willing company in lonely places and at home, I could not have been able to accomplish so much.

I was also relieved of the burden of looking after my widowed mother, when my nephew, Ravindra, and my sister-in-law, *Bhabhi*, willingly relieved me of this duty. Hence, from my student days till today, even ordinary family chores have not in any way prevented me from doing my normal work of reading and writing. My sedentary habits would have ruined my health had I not been early in life accustomed to doing some household chores in our Bombay home—such as washing clothes, sweeping floor and so on. I had also formed the habit of getting up early, fetching milk from the *kotha* (local dairy) going down four storeys almost every morning and preparing tea not only for myself but for the entire family. This habit became so much a part of my life that later when students had accompanied me to Junnar and other caves, I would prepare tea not only for myself but also for them. Short visits to the Christian Ashram at Kodaikanal, and Shri Aurobindo Ashram at Pondicherry taught me and my wife the dignity of manual work.

Naturally therefore we never found it difficult to

do all our personal work when we were out on tour. This habit became a positive assest when after retirement we had to look after our own garden, no college *māli* being available. My wife, in fact, had developed this garden. For when we shifted to our present premises (Sat-chit-ananda) there was not a blade of grass to be found anywhere. The ground was rocky. But when the house began to be built, she gradually transplaned the plants and trees that we had grown during our ten years stay at Bungalow No. 3. Some of these trees were no less than seven or eight feet high. People who saw her carrying these plants wondered how they would survive transplantation. But every plant survived. The barren place has now been turned into a lush grove.

But the 5,000 sq. ft. garden-cum-grove is to be maintained. At first, I began watering with a plastic pipe. This also took considerable time and effort, walking up and down the garden several times. In February when trees would shed leaves and large heaps of leaves would be found scatteted in the lawn. "Should I sweep them of ?" I wondered. "What would happen, if some one sees me sweeping?" This small vanity I could soon overcome and I regularly started sweeping the nooks and corners of our garden and it appeard therefore always spick and span. This exercise involing at least six hours of work, particularly during summer months, did not in any way distract me from my work. Nor was my writing suffered as is evident from the number of books published during the last four years.

8

Just as I had one or two unpleasant experiences during our exploration tours, so there were some very pleasant experiences as well. One of them I should like to relate.

During Christmas holidays 1940, I had taken four students—Naik, Patil, Mehendale, Bengare—to see the monuments in the Nizam's territory particularly with a view to teaching Bengari how to study the sculptures and images of Ellora. This study formed a part of my planned study of the Deccan monuments dynastywise. Unfortunately the plan could not fructify as the Director of Archaeology did not permit us to carry out the study because he told me that they would themselves carry out the plan. Thirty-six years have passed since then but they were still planning to undertake some such study. No scholar has so far carried out the kind of study I had contemplated. The late Dr Gupte did some work but his was of a general nature.

As usual, my wife had also accompanied me on this trip. Since we did not know anybody at Hyderabad, we had to put up in a small dirty hotel in the heart of the city. There are a number of Gujarati merchants in Hyderabad. As my wife and all of us lodged amidst them, a Gujarati business-man—his name I forget now—inquired as to who we were and what we were doing there. I told him the nature of our mission. He pointed out : "If you are Professor and this lady is your wife why do you not go to Shri Chandulal Dangoria?" So this businessman took me to Dangoria. Shri Chandulal was an engineer in the Improvement Board and was known for his hospitality. He and the members of his family not only welcomed me and my wife but my four students as well. Then he took us round Hyderabad in his car for three or four days. He gave us letters of introduction to his engineer friends at Palampet and other sites.

We were all overhelmed by Chandulal's hospitality. Since then we have become life-long friends. In fact, he is one of the few friends that we have. Such hospitality has now become a thing of the past. It was quite normal then, particularly in a rich "native" or princely state, when the officers and nobility would be living in large, commodious houses having one or two large guest-rooms.

The guests would then be always welcome. In fact,
to have guests was itself the sign of nobility. Now
owing to various reasons which need not be discussed
here we have become self-centred and hospitality has
become a thing of the past.

7

Whether one believes in astrology partly or in
full, there is some ground for thinking that my life
as well as those of others cannot be purely deter-
mind by ourselves. Some positive steps in developing interest in archaeology I must have taken but
I believe all these opportunities came one after
another according to some pre-determined pattern
of which I was not the author. I however could
not rest satisfied with this attitude. I was eager to
verify astrological predictions, particularly regarding
our future through a proper scientific inquiry. I
have therefore taken a few steps in this direction.

While the forecast in the *Bhrigu Samhitā* was
forthright and unequivocal, two other samhitas —
Satya or *Sūrya* and *Saptarshi* -- which I recently consulted, had made similar predictions about my life, the
last even said that I would discover Lanka. It
also said that Lankā was at the centre (*kendra*) of
Bharata and not outside ! Thus, these so-called
samhitas, if authentic and not fake, as some indeed
are, do contain into predictions which would astound
anyone. They also make him inquire the basis of this
knowledge and the reasons why the knowledge was
reduced to writing at all.

The *Nadi Granthas* of the South are similar
samhitas, though I have no personal experience of
these books. But I could vouchsafe for their authen-
ticity on the testimony of two of my colleagues. In
the South the owner actually hands over the leaf or
leaves to the persons concerned saying that he has
no further use of them.

My experience of the astrologers, though not much, has been equally encouraging. The first one had predicted, as far back as 1939, that a high Government honour would be conferred on me; another said that I would leave behind "imperishable fame", while a famous business man, who happened to be an amateur palmist, looking casually at my palm remarked, as far back as 1938, that I would do "fine work".

Thus, there is little doubt in my mind that astrology, call it by whatever name you like, is a science or an intuitive discipline. As a subject, it is worthwhile investigating and deserving to be put on a more secure foundation, so that it may help us in choosing a proper vocation and thus incidentally save some waste of human capital.

First, we should ascertain whether these are "freak" truths. If not, then it should be broad-based like all true knowledge. It must pass through all the scientific tests that we can think of. We should have a reasonable number of samples from each *samhitā* : *Bhrigu*, *Satya* or *Sūrya*, *Saptarshi*, and *Nadi Granthas*. These samples should be verifiable. Further, if the *Samhitā* predictions are found reliable we should tape-record these and photograph them also, if possible, for proper study.

Besides we should have a comprehensive list of all the *samhitas* and *Nadi Granthas*, of which some are now in private possession, but a large number is acquiring dust in public libraries of Baroda, Calcutta, Jaipur, Mysore, Pune, and Travancore, as well as in Kashmir and Nepal. The catalogue of these *samhitas* itself would be an independent research project, entailing considerable travel all over India besides expertise and, above all, aptitude. But meanwhile the existing and known *samhitas* could be utilised. From amongst these, the fake ones have to be eliminated. Such fake *samhitas* do exist. I myself was instrumental in detecting one at Pune.

A scientific study of the known *samhitas* and *Nadi Granthas* can be undertaken only with the cooperation of the owners of the *samhitas*. At present, these are regarded as sacrosanct and "untouchable", to be handled and read only by the owners, some of whom belong to old Brahmin families. While the ascertaining of the reliability of these *samhitas* might boost up the business of some astrologers, (though it is already a flourishing business), some other *samhitas* if found to be not so reliable, are likely to be discredited, and thus the owners would lose their business.

The *Saṁhitā* owners must come forword and allow their manuscripts to be photographed or tape-recorded. Besides we shall also need the cooperation of the persons whose lives are thus proposed to be scientifically studied. Not only should they be willing to help check the readings in these *samhitas*, but permit the use of their personal data so collected. Of course, the investigator would take all possible care in keeping the data confidential, thuse reducing the possibility of identifying the persons so studied.

Studies such as these entail considerable expenditure and outside cooperation. Both these might not be easily available. At the Deccan College therefore we have undertaken, at present, a limited inquiry. This has shown considerable promise. Thus we are also studying subjects other than archaeology.

A study of thirty-four horoscopes of teachers, students and technical assistants in our Department of Archaeology has shown that Saturn is the ruling planet of persons who are intimately connected with any aspect of archaeology—excavators, photographers, and draftsmen. Saturn is weak or low if the persons' interests are peripherial. This has nothing to do with the person's status which is ruled by planets like Jupiter and Mars. These again must be in particular houses, such as the second, sixth or tenth from the point of view of profession, and in the fourth and fifth houses from the point of view of education and research. The study of 34 horoscopes revealed that the main ruling planets of those who are connected with archaeology are: Saturn, Jupiter, Mars, and Mercury.

In 14 out of 34 cases (42%) analysed, Saturn was found to be in its exalted *mulatrikona* position or in its own sign namely, Libra, Aquarius, and Capricorn. In 13 other cases (39%) it was found to occupy its friendly signs such as those ruled by Mercury, Venus, and Jupiter. In the remaining 7 cases (19%) it was found to occupy its inimical or unfriendly signs such as those ruled by Mars, Sun, and Moon respectively. However Jupiter, Mars, and Mercury have been found to play their role in relation to Saturn when they are considered from the point of research and excavations. We have thus made a modest beginning in our study of astrology. Not only should the result be broad-based, but we should study horoscopes of others—preferably those of the doctors, engineers and scientists and see whether we can arrive at the same conclusions positively as well as negatively.

The scientific approach while it may prove the truth of astrology and establish it as a fairly reliable discipline would raise other problems as well. Why did these *samhitā* writers or seers make these predictions, about all persons—high and low? Did they derive any earthly benefit? Possibly none. Was it then a purely academic exercise? The aim of astrology should not be to strengthen our fatalism but to find a method of guiding our men and women to select a vocation or a profession for which they are most suited by nature. There are other applications as well, as, for instance, life insurance. Besides many of our superstitions, particularly the one about the New Moon Day—*Amāvasyā*—which is generally thought to be a bad day for the seriously ill can be methodically examined by collecting staistics in respect of the number of deaths occurring on these

7

My attitude to awards national and/or states as
also awards of various academic societies and institutions, was formed by one sentence from *King Lear*
which I studied in my B.A. class. The sentence was
"Ripeness is all". I had understood the expression in
the light of one verse from the *Gita* which is: *Karmanye
vadhika kareste ne phalesu kadacana* (you are expected
to perform your duty without caring for the fruits).
I was told only a few years ago by a Professor of
Marathi in the Pune University that Shakespearean
scholars do not interpret the line in the way I have
done. Anyway *Ripeness in all* has been the guiding
motto in my life. Hence I have never attempted to
canvass for any honour such as presidentship of this
or that conference, membership of this or that body
in the university or elsewhere. Nor do I canvass
for this or that prize. Here I would say that 'can-
vassing' is different from an inquiry about its nature
or requirements for this or that prize. Nor did I crave
for the state or national awards. Somehow or other
I have always felt or desired—and this may be attri-
buted to some kind of pride or vanity or simply human weakness—that the award should come to me
without my prior knowledge. Only then would I
derive real joy from an award. This has happened
four or five times in my life, but none gave me more
surprise than the award of the *Padma Bhushan*.

As I have said earlier, it was predicted long ago,
as far back as 1935 by a yonng teacher, who was an
amateur astrologer that some national award like
knighthood would be conferred upon me because my
horoscope happened to be like that of one of distinguished relatives of Sarla. An amateur palmist had
also foretold of a similar honour.

I was, therefore, wondering how and when such

prophecies would be fulfilled, when every year on the Republic Day one heard on the radio honours being conferred on this or that person. Four years ago my wife happened to hear such an announcement, and asked me why some such honour was not awarded to me. I said, "I do not know but it is not in my hand to advise the authrities". Then three years ago, around *Diwali* an amateur astrologer friend of mine had come to my house. Before leaving he said, "Some national honour is bound to be conferred on you during this year, because your *Guru* (Jupiter) is exalted!" However, no enquiries were made at the state or national level, which I am told is often done, before an honour is conferred.

In 1974 I left for Kerala to deliver lectures at the Cochin and Trivandrum Universities on the 18th January on behalf of the University Grants Commission. I had already retired as Professor and Director of the Deccan College on 10th December 1973. At Cochin after delivering three lectures, my pupil, John and a few of his students and I left for seeing the megalithic monuments and cave engravings. On reaching the cave in the afternoon, after strenuous walking and most difficult climbing, we found that it was impossible to go further as evening was drawing near. So instead of returning to Cochin, we passed the night at a nearby place. The next day, early in the morning, we left for the cave, climbed it with the greatest difficulty and came back to Cochin late at night. Then we were informed that a trunk call had been made from New Delhi for me. I thought that it should be about some UGC meeting.

Next day—the Republic Day—we left by a jeep for Ernakulam. Here John and I lunched in a modern tourist-type hotel. There was a kiosk where newspapers were sold. I asked John if he could buy an English newspaper. He brought a copy of the *Indian Express*. After going through all other news, I took a glance at the list of awards, and to my great

surprise, I found my name next that of the late
Dr Moti Chandra among the people who were awarded the Padma Bhushan. I showed it to John and
he also confirmed that there was no mistake. But
mistakes do take place. We have exprience of our
Universities and State Boards of Education when
every year at least five mistakes occur when results
are declared.

Since I had no previous intimation from new
Delhi, until I left Pune on the 18th, I was indeed
wondering if there was any mistake! My wonder
grew when I reached Trivandrum. The Professor,
who had come to receive me, said nothing about the
award. Next day also he was silent. I wanted some
independent confirmation about the award. This
could not be done even at Bangalore. When I reached Bangalore on the 29th Dr Nagaraja Rao, my
former pupil and then the Director or Archaeology,
met me at the station but said nothing. I was,
therefore, afraid of breaking the news to him. Nor
did I ask him to find out whether it was true. It
was in this mood that I left Bangalore. At Dharwar,
however, my suspense was over when Dr Sundara
met me with an invitation to a function arranged in
my honour.

At Pune a trunk call was first received in the
main office of the Deccan College from New Delhi
on the 24th or 25th. A second call was received by
my wife at my residence, when the person enquired
if I would receive the award. She replied that I was
not at Pune but she would be glad to receive the
award on my behalf, if desired. This news she passed
on to the Director, who naturally questioned her
about the genuinenss of the telephonic message,
and asked her to wait till a confirmation was received by a telegram or a letter.

I am reminded of a similar situation when in 1961
or so, our Vice-Chancellor and the Chairman of the
council of Management, Prof. D.G. Karve, received a

100   telegram, apparently meant for Dr D.K. Karve, conferring the Bharat Ratna on him. Now the persons, who were handling this affair at New Delhi, should have known the current address of the person on whom they were conferring the highest honour of the nation. The episode is narrated in detail, as it has a little comic aspect but then such are the ways of life.

A similar incident had happened a few years earlier. A Society in Bombay had decided to award me the Dadabhoy Nowrojee Prize of Rs. 3,000. They informed me on an ordinary sheet of paper about this, and also asked me to collect the Prize at Bombay on a certain day. I had never heard of this Society nor of the Prize. But the amount of the prize was fairly large. I wondered if it was not a practical joke! A few months ago the famous Asiatic Society of Bombay informed me that they had decided to award the Campbell Gold Medal to me. The decision was taken more than a year-and-a-half ago, but they had forgotten to inform me!

However, of all the awards which I got, I value most the Bruce Foote Plaque awarded to me by the Anthropology Department of the Calcutta University. As Kalidasa has said long ago that it was always better to receive a gift or get one's wishes fulfilled from persons who are more qualified.

Therefore, I also welcomed the invitation from the Wenner Gren Foundation to participate in the symposium on Urbanization at Burg Wartenstein, in 1960 and then later an invitation to participate in the symposium on homo sapiens at Paris in 1967. I was also glad to receive the invitation to participate in the symposium on the Philosophy of Archaeology at Flagstaff, Arizona and the "Palaeolithic of Asia" at Montreal and Chicago. I also responded warmly to the invitation to preside over the First Maharashtra Itihasa Conference. Likewise I was also glad when I was elected unanimously the President of the

All these occasions gave me real joy. On such
occasions I felt that whatever had happened had happened because one intrinsically deserved it. Some of
my friends, whose experience has been otherwise, have
questioned the wisdom of this philosophy. My reply
to this can only be that I had formed the philosophy
of my life much before any success came to me, basing
my philosophy upon my experience of the first-year
examination of the Inter Arts course.   Mathematics
and physics were my weak points.   In the latter I
got only six marks in the practical out of 30 in the
annual examination. This had really frightened me.
Instead of depending upon tips from my friends, I
relied on the advice given by Principal Katti the
previous year.   Intensive reading and writing paid
and I secured more than 60 per cent marks in physics and mathematics and a high second class in the
aggregate in the Inter-Arts Examination.

8

Here I may also say a few words as to my attitude to prayer, worship of images and God in general.
Our family has been traditionally the follower of
Vallabhacharya School of Vaishnavism. The principal tenet of this school is to have unqualified faith in
Shri Krishna. The images and paintings of Krishna's
boyhood are worshipped in various forms requiring
complete surrender and offering of everything one
has including oneself to the Divine.   Moreover the
devotee is also required not to worship any other
god. Nor should he observe ritualistic fast on Mon-
days, Tuesdays or Saturdays. Belief in Krishna and
Krishna alone in preference to all other gods and
godesses is to be found clearly explained in the *Gita*,
but this was re-stated and made a way of life by
Shri Vallabhacharya who was inspired by the *Gītā*
and the *Bhāgavata*. The one-directional devotion to
Sri Krishna made all of us, members of the family

particularly, fearless. We did not go to the temple of any other god.

Naturally, from a very early age I had my own niche in which I kept Sri Krishna's painting and worshipped it every morning after bathing. I also read the *Gītā* and knew it almost by heart. The *Bhāgavata* was read daily at home. Now I know that all this was done mechanically, more out of habit than out of devotion. But it did build up in me an unshakable faith in the Divine Force. I always read Vallabhacharya's verse which said, "Do not be afraid of anything, but have faith in me and leave your fears to me."

One day, when I was in the sixth standard, my mother was taken suddenly very ill. At that time I felt like offering my prayer to Vinadhari Krishna at play whose photo we had hung in our office room. My prayer was so sincere, so heart-felt that I had no doubt that it would be answered. The other occasion when my prayer was heard is worth relating. That was some four years ago. I was at that time the Director of the Institute and a private film-maker had planned to make a documentary film about the Deccan College. Since the late Lokmanya Bal Gangadhar Tilak had been the student at the Deccan College, it had been arranged to film the room where he was taught For this purpose the film-maker had arranged a small function in front of the room. On this occasion Tilak's grandson was to be the chief guest, and the then Vice-Chancellor of the Pune University had previously agreed to be present. The function was scheduled on August 1 at 8 a.m. and the local members of the Council of the Management, Trustees and others had been invited.

However, just two or three days before the function was to take place, the Vice-Chancellor asked me to cancel the function because he thought that he should have been invited as the chief guest and not Tilak's grandson. He felt that it was a downright insult to his august position.   103

I was in a great fix.   Considering the great es-
teem in which Tilak is held all over India, and particularly in Maharashtra, it was indeed ridiculous to
cancel the function.   So both my predecessor and
myself went to request the Vice-Chancellor but we
were told that he had left Pune and would not return before three or four days. Apart from the great
expenses which the film-maker had incurred, it was
difficult to withdraw the invitation.

Not knowing what to do I went to our "bedroom-
temple".   Here we had installed a fine marble image
of Gopala Krishna and a statue of Sri Upasani
Maharaj made by my wife when she was student of
the Diploma Class in Modelling in the J. J. School
of Art in Bombay. Besides, there were photographs
of the saints such as Sri Aurobindo, the Mother,
Ramana Maharshi, Sai Baba, and Satya Sai Baba
about whom we had read and had some first-hand
experience.

What was needed was a miracle—a change of
heart on the part of the Vice-Chancellor. And it
was that I prayed for and my prayer was answered.
Just twenty-four hours before the function was to be
held, a telephone massage came from the Vice-
Chancellor saying that he would be present and that
I should not cancel the function.

Except the film-maker we had not informed anybody about the cancellation of the function. He and
his film unit were staying somewhere at Deccan
Gymkhana. So our Estate Manager was sent post-
haste to inform him of the latest development.   Fortunately he had not left.   He came with his entire
unit as well as the chief guest. The Vice-Chancellor
did come and everything passed off well.

I did not know then but I learnt later that the
various Rigvedic gods were nothing but the manifes-

tations of Nature. Still later when I studied iconography and particularly Tantric Siddhis I came to
know how various idols, some benign and some
terrible, were worshipped because of man's fear of
the unseen and unknown. Many gods and goddesses
were also adored due to sectarian rivalries. As a
result, my faith in idol-worship diminished and I
gave up the daily worship—called *Sevā*—though I
had still faith in the Divine Element.

Neither my father nor any member of our family,
had paid obeisance to a saint, though my father
during his younger days had a great fascination for
Theosophy. However, my attitude changed when I
came into contact with Sri Upasani Maharaj of
Sakori, then Sri Aurobindo and the Mother and
later Ramana Maharshi. After joining the Deccan
Collage, during one of our tours we happened to go
to Pondichery and Tiruvannamalai. At both places
we were much impressed by the emphasis on meditation. The significance of Sri Aurobindo's complete
surrender to God was slowly revealed to us in the
course of our repeated visits to the *āshram*. The
"surrender" is to be practised by devoting all our
day-to-day actions to God.

It was at this time (in 1943, to be precise) that
we spent some three weeks at the Christian *āshram*
at Kodaikanal. Here I was impressed by the way
all the work was done by the inmates of the Ashram
themselves. Thus in one way or the other our life
was being influenced more and more by the abstract
spiritual principles.

This was given a more definite turn by Sri Upasani Maharaj when I visited his *āshram* at Sakori.
I had participated in *pūjās* both at home and in
Vaishnava temples. I like *bhajans* and *kīrtans* to be
performed in a quiet way. At Sakori right from
4 a. m. until late at night, excepting a few hours of
rest for midday meals, there was some *puja* or the
other and the bells would ring all the time. Though

I participated in these public *āratis* in the beginning, I could not stand these, and once or twice even spoke to Sri Upasani Maharaj about my discomfiture, brought up as I was in the atmosphere of quiet, personal *sevā* at home. He told me that each person had a different background. For a large number of people the mass *pūjā* was good, because it helped them to think of God but meditation and the like was neant for the very few.

This is certainly true. For the common man does require something concrete, some object, some image on which to fasten upon, though it is true that we in India, like the Catholics and some other denominations in the West, have overdone the religious practices. In fact, it is all due to our varied desires and increasing wants and fears. Hence the Buddha was right, when he said one should check one's *vasanas*. Desire will vanish and with it also belief in anthropomorphic gods. Hence he refused to say anything about god because, in the ultimate analysis, god exists only as long as you have a desire.

I think that this was the greatest discovery that the Buddha had made. His was indeed a Realization. I do not think that the Upanishads have put this matter as explicity as he did. It is this truth which the *Gita* had further elaborated and explained in simple words which have been explained with apt illustrations time and again by our saints. Thus Upasani Baba's repeated insistance on the suppresion of *ahamkāra* can be understood if we resolve to do all our manual work ourselves. Once our ego is suppressed, our wants decrease, and as the wants decrease and are gradually eliminated, the final realization—oneness with ourselves—call it god it you will, is not distant. Of course, the final step is the most difficult step. Many saints and *siddhas* have faltered here and having failed got into the stream of *saṁsāra* again. I, therefore, believe in the theory of *karma*, and all the religious paths, high and low, had advocated for its conquest. For each one of us acts and thinks according to one's past *karma* and has to continually strive to get over the bondage of *karma*. If, therefore, I bow before a saint, it is because I feel the need for a *guru* in my spiritual life as much as in mundane life and a saint like Sri Upasani Maharaj who has by precept and example achieved the Divine, can certainly show me the way. And I have seen from my own example that what is needed for success is faith in one's *guru* and hard work. Mere faith does not lead us anywhere.

Seven

Archaeology for the Masses

1. *Quarrels and Controversies*   2. *Dr Kosambi*
3. *Interesting Incidents*   4. *Archaeology for the People* 5. *Marathi and Hindi Writings*

NORMALLY scholars, I am told, avoid controversies. But I could not and as I said at the outset, I began my academic career with a vitriolic attack made against me by one of my teachers, Professor Shembavaekar as far back as 1929-30. Ten years later, after returning from England, I wrote a paper on "Gujarat Epigraphy" for the *Journal of the Bombay University*. The paper was severely criticised by Shri A.S. Gadre who was then an Assistant in the Baroda Department of Archaeology. I had never heard of this gentleman. Nor did I know that he was going to be the Director of Archaeology in future. Gadre imagined that I was his rival for had I not returned from England with a Ph.D. and that too on Gujarat archaeology! However before publishing Gadre's criticism the Editor sought my reply which I gave. But when the editorial board saw my reply, they thought of dropping both the articles.

Gadre had to come into my contact some ten years later many times in one capacity or the other. He was asked to look after our Gujarat expedition, making all arrangements for camp, food, labourers, and so on. He was very courteous to me though, I think, he was envious of my superior position as

108 the leader of several Gujarat expeditions. We remained friends nevertheless. As the Director of the Department of Archaeology of Baroda he published my report to which he contributed a small preface for which I am grateful to him. Gadre died a few years ago.

There was another scholar from Gujarat, the late A. V. Pandya. Though he was apparently very friendly, he circulated adverse reports about me in Gujarat. Two of them I should like to mention. He said on one occasion that the human skeletons found by us at Langhanj were those of children and hence my conclusion was questionable. He also claimed that the report of the first Gujarat prehistoric expedition was entirely written by him. Naturally these canards had to be promptly contradicted and I had no other choice but to call his bluff in the Ahmedabad newspapers, though there are some scholars who still believe that it was Pandya who had actually drafted the Gujarat expeditions report, not I. As the subsequent development in perhistory in India speaks for itself I need not dilate on this subject.

Pandya died four months ago, and I am glad to say that when I met him last at Vallabha Vidya Nagar and later dined with him, I found that all ill-feelings had vanished. I was so happy that we parted as friends. Not only Pandya but also the small land of prehistorians in distant Bengal, constantly fed by Pandya's adverse reports, had begun to regard me as an upstart. And upstart I certainly was. Had I not written a Ph. D. thesis on 'historic' archaeology and was not prehistory outside the domain of my specialisation?" So when a famous Professor of geography and prehistory from Bengal criticised my views in the *Journal of the Asiatic Society* naturally I had to give a reply. The reply was entitled "Is Soan a Flake Industry?" After the publication of this article no criticism was heard from this quarter. These canards and criticisms however had

no impact on me. I always did my work unconcer-
ned, exploring newer and newer areas, and guiding
my students who came from different parts of India,
far and near. So when I met this Bengali critic of
mine, face to face, in Gauhati, where I spoke on my
discovery in Kashmir, I had to ask him point-blank if
he would like to comment on my discovery. The
Bengali critic kept quiet.

I had my moments of joy as well. One of the
greatest joys in my life was when the Department of
Anthropology conferred on me the first Bruce Foote
Plaque, (of which the late Professor was an active
member) in recognition of my services to prehistory.
I think this honour was of greater value than what
I have received before or after because I got it from
my critics who had, as time passed, turned into my
admirers.

<h3 style="text-align:center">2</h3>

I also think it to be a great honour to be complimented by no less a person than Professor D.D.
Kosambi. As is well known to many scholars, he
had mercilessly criticised the first edition of my book
Prehistory and Proto-history of India and Pakistan in the
Times of India. When I read it, I wrote to him (and
also in the *Times of India*) that his criticism was all
misplaced. I then invited him to our museum at the
Deccan College. After some initial hesitation he
came, and was fully convinced about the soundness of
my researches. However, he wondered why I had
not cared to see his discoveries in and around Pune.
I did. At the end of the next day, he said before
parting, "I am glad that an archaeologist of your
calibre had at last seen my work and also promised to
continue to work on them." Though he died soon
after this meeting, we at the Institute kept our
promise. We also brought out a book which we
dedicated to his memory. Thus, one after another,
controversies, some of which were purely personal,
died down. But given my nature, I cannot avoid

controversies. I will always revolt against can't and make-belief.

3

Criticisms apart, I had to face many difficult situations during the long course of my field-work. There were times when the workers threatened to boycott the work that I had undertaken. Often no local workmen could be found if the area to be excavated were situated in an agricultural region. Again at times in places where untouchability was practised, outsiders like us were ostracised and denied food, shelter, and even drinking water.

Let me relate a few such incidents. At Kolhapur, among our workmen there was a real *Draupadi*, probably belonging to the Mang or Mahar community. Though very dark, unlike the usual Marathi women, her beauty charmed our labourers. Some of the local male workers began to take liberty with her which I learned later is not unusual among these communities. This had to be stopped, I thought. When the person concerned did not listen to my warnings, I had to dismiss him. But with his dismissal the entire workers struck work. Though this was quite unexpected, I was not frightened. We wound up our equipment and carried them to our camp which fortunately was not very far. Next day we decided to work without assistants in one trench only. At the end of the day, the workers realized their folly and one by one all joined work.

At Akhaj, a village near Langhnaj, and later at the famous Harappan site of Rangpur, and also during our first excavation at Jorwe, near Sangamner, we found that the workers were not available for manual labour. I told my colleage Dr M.G. Dikshit, who was my only companion at that time (1947-48), that we should ourselves start digging with a pickaxe, shovel and *gamela*. The labourers who refused to be hired thought this to be a great fun,

and some of them collected near our one and only
trench. But some of the onlookers took pity on us
seeing us struggle with a pickaxe and shovel. First
one, then another, joined our skeleton party. Within
a week, a sizable group of workers—mostly untou-
chables—who have normally no work at the end of
March started working with us joyously. Joyously
because whether in Gujarat or Maharashtra or in
Madhya Pradesh, Andhra and Karnataka wherever
we had excavated our relations with the workers had
always been cordial. Not only did we have perfect
understanding with one and all but, above all, since
one of us personally supervised the weekly disburs-
ment of wages there was no occasion when the
labourers could complain that they were cheated or
underpaid.

A Hirpura we had a nasty experience. We were
only two —Dr Karve and I. Since we know that no
local worker could be found, we asked two of our
Langhnaj workers to accompany us. Everyone knew
me at Hirpura as I had stayed there for a few days
in 1941. But now nobody even cared to offer us
shelter for a night or offer us cooked food because
we had left our cook at Langhnaj. The reason for
this total social boycott was that among our two
workmen one was a semi-untouchable! The consequence was that after a day's walk along the Sabarmati
in search of sections, Dr Karve had to cook
in our small room with fuel which had gone wet.
Though it is now more than thirty-six years that
this unhappy incident had taken place, untouchability is still practised in villages in India.

As I have said in the preceding pages, my health
being what it is, I can ill-afford to take liberties
with my food or drink. Even an extra cup of tea,
I had to refuse when offered on numerous
occasions by our hosts. On one occasion when
after a long walk from Hodol we reached Dharoi,
late at night, with our camp followers and equipment, we found to our great surprise that the only

place where we could stay, a school room, had been closed for the week-end. We were advised to find shelter in a garage on the river bank. Unfortunately there was a truck inside the garage which carried kaolin from the local quarry. So some of us had to sleep in the truck, and others lay under it. As it was already quite late our cook gave us what he could cook in a trice which turned out to be *khichadi*, a melange of pulse and rice. I hesitated. Dr Karve, who was a hard taskmaster and a dour disciplinarian hurled a lecture at me. When she did not stop for some time, I quietly remarked, "Dear Mrs. Karve, don't you know, that you are a palaeolith and I am a microlith". This was the most apposite simile that I could think of, for in every way she was different from all of us. But I never imagined that this remark would sting her like a thorn. It haunted her that whole night and for many years which I later on came to know when I narrated this incident to M. C. Burkitt, the doyen of British pre-historians who had invited both of us to lunch at his house in Cambridge in 1951-52. Dr Karve then said, "Your retorts are very painful. They directly hit at one's weak spot". Dr Karve was right because two of my ruling stars are Sagittarius and Scorpion.

4

It is said that scholars and scientists love to live in ivory towers. Not only do they not care to share their knowledge with the public, they regard it as sacrilege to gain cheap popularity. This attitude might have had some justification when we held ideas quite different from what we hold today about our duties towards society. Whatever be the reasons of this attitude, I have not cared to find them out. I can speak for myself and say that I do not like to dwell in ivory towers and that I never held back any new knowledge I had acquired or discovered. I had always shared what knowledge I had gained with my colleagues and students and also with the public

I have already mentioned above how I was impelled to write my first research paper on *Kuṇḍa-māla* and *Uttararāmacharita*. It was the same desire which made me translate into Gujarati a long article on the Indus Civilization which was published in *Indian Historical Quarterly* as far back as in 1932. It was in this spirit that I welcomed an opportunity to lecture to the children of a village school in Gujarat about our work on the Sabarmati. And when I spoke to them on the history of the pen-knife for some fifteen minutes, my colleagues were indeed surprised to find that a subject like palaeoliths and microliths could even interest the illiterate villagers !

This and other incidents led me to organize exhibitions soon after our excavations were over or even when they were in progress at Kolhapur, Nasik-Nevasa, Ahar, Tripuri, and Inamgaon. I mentioned this idea in a lecture that I had delivered to the Department of Sociology in the Bombay University in 1938. I also wrote an article to this effect which the *Illustrated Weekly* published under the title: "Archaeology for the Masses." In that article I had said that before undertaking the excavation of a site it was our duty to tell the people of that area in their own language why we were excavating and after the excavation was completed it was our duty to explain to them what we had found and what new knowledge our excavation had contributed.

Fortunately, the authorities of the Deccan College—especially our Director and the Council of Management—had no objection to this "new concept of educating" the people at Kolhapur, Nasik and Nevasa, though, unfortunately, my idea cut no ice with the ASI. But outside, my idea caught the imagination of the people. I was indeed surprised when we visited Kalibangan in Ganga Nagar district (Rajasthan). The principal of a local college came running to me and requested me to give a lec-

114   ture in his village, when he learnt that I was paying a visit to the site. However, much I would have wished to enlighten the students and the teachers about the contribution made by the site to our knowledge of the Indus Civilization, I could not think of committing the breach of professional behaviour because this duty rightly belonged to the scholars who had been conducting excavations on that site since 1961.

Is it not a pity that the people in whose area we are excavating should not know what is happening? On the contrary they would be proud of their village or town if they were told that their distant ancestors were not uncivilized as they are commonly made to imagine. Compare the ignorance in Rajasthan with the knowledge that every village schoolboy has in Western Maharashtra about his distant past, because we had acquainted them with our excavations through the newspapers, *Sakal* and *Kesari* as well as by distributing booklets about the excavations at Nevasa and Inamgaon.

Hence, we were not surprised, when a fisherman at Kalegaon on the Godavari, an out-of-the-way village in Nagar district, on seeing Dr Ansari and me in his village enquired if we had come in search of fossil bones of animals. He then led us to a site on the river bank where he had seen an odd thing in his childhood. This turned out, after hours of careful excavation, a prized find—one of the most intact specimens which we named *Bos Namadicus*. It is now one of the valued objects of the Indian Museum in Calcutta.

At Nevasa, we had called a meeting of village teachers and given them a couple of potsherds and explained to them their cultural significance and then told them to look for sites where these could be found. The result was that every year, we got letters from some village teachers and others informing us about the antiquities they had sighted in their villages.

In addition to these site exhibitions, booklets and lectures, I was keen that we should have text-books on various aspects of archaeology in Marathi. I am glad to say that under the Chairman-ship of Professor S. B. Deo, my colleagues at the Deccan College have now written books on art and architecture, numismatics, epigraphy and palaeography in Marathi. Dr Deo himself had written a very exhaustive book on archaeology in general.

5

While I wrote with considerable ease in English, and also in Gujarati, the latter being my mother tongue, I never wrote in Marathi. However, after our excavations at Nasik sometime in 1950-51, Dr M. G. Dikshit asked me to contribute an article for his Marathi magazine *Prasad*. This was how I began writing in Marathi. It is not difficult, particularly when one knows Sanskrit, and has learnt to speak Marathi and Hindi from childhood. But this know-ledge is not sufficient for writing articles in good Marathi or Hindi. However, I did make an attempt, first in Marathi and later in Hindi. I found that the best away was to dictate in Marathi or Hindi to a person preferably a scholar of these languages. In this way I could easily and quickly explain my thoughts instead of the scholar trying to translate the article into Marathi or Hindi.

Amongst the scholars who helped me and, in fact, encouraged me to write in Marathi, I must mention P. R. Kulkarni. First, he himself started by transla-ting my articles and then he persuaded me to write. In this way several articles were written which I contributed to *Sakal* and *Kesari*. Now this is being done with the assistance of Vasanti Joshi. When *Dharmayug* approached me for articles in Hindi, I contributed several articles with the help of Dr Malati Nagar. Of late, Jethmal, a scholar from Bikaner, has taken to translating into Hindi on his

116 own my articles published in Gujarati. Thus in one
way or another I have never refrained from dis-
seminating knowlege or information about archaeology.

Eight

Future of Indian Archaeology

*1. Deccan College Museum 2. Language Issue,
Cow Slaughter and other allied matters 3. Future
of Indian Archaeology 4. New Archaeology 5. Guiding Research 6. Champion of Lost Cause 7. Sanskrit Dictionary.*

WHILE exhibitions, that I organized, educated a
layman, the exhibits can be useful to a student of
archaeology only if they are housed in a museum.
That is to say, unless the scholars have access to a
museum no real progress can be made in our knowledge of the past. Therefore, to have a museum I
began modestly by spreading on my table the potsherds that we gathered from the mediaeval site of
Vijayanagar, which I had visited with my students
in 1940. When Rao Bahadur Dikshit saw these potsherds, spread out on my large table, which I had
inherited from the Satara museum when it was shifted to the Deccan College, he had a hearty laugh
and wondered what I was going to do with these
potsherds. But perhaps Rao Bahadur Dikshit did
not realize that if these were systematically collected,
they would tell us the shapes of vessels which people
used including the kings and princes of yore. At
present, we know next to nothing about their domes-
tic life. We displayed copies of these potshreds in
large wall show-cases as well as the estampages of
inscriptions from the caves of Junnar taken by Naik
and Patil. Thus the true copies of 2000-year-old ins-

criptions were exhibited in our college which were indeed useful for teaching palaeography to our M.A. students.

However, within two years, these and other large show-cases had to make room for the palaeoliths, microliths, and bone implements from Gujarat, and the various maps and river sections, of which excellent coloured copies were made by Amrit Pandya. Also exhibited were human skeletons and large animal fossils from Langhnaj. I was indeed lucky to find enough space to house them as well as furniture, large and small show-cases and tables, as if specially ordered in anticipation of our finds from Gujarat. Very few institutions—colleges and offices of the Survey—have this facility. The furniture that we had acquired, though not quite or exactly suitable for artistic or scientific display, was good enough for display of the exhibits.

During those years the Deccan College had neither the means nor the money to buy museum equipments. But when we shifted to our old premises across the river, we dug at Nasik and carried out our river-surveys in Andhra and Karnataka, antiquities of all kinds began to pour in. These had to be stored and a few of them were required to be exhibited.

Help came from one of the then Education Ministers, Shri Dinkarrao Desai. Paying a visit to our museum and seeing it crowded with antiquities, he immediately sanctioned an *ad hoc* grant of Rs. 15,000 for new show-cases. Unfortunately, these had to be designed like the old furniture to go well with the furniture that we had. Thus, as far as the show-cases were concerned, I could not get modern or up-to-date show-cases as some of my younger colleagues and students desired I should. But the old furniture could not be ignored. In the museums in England, for example, not everything was destroyed during the Second World War and when new additions were made these had to be designed like the old ones. In Germany, for instance, they could start afresh, building and furniture having been completely destroyed, and thus made their museums look completely modern. When we shifted to the Deccan College campus, our Department was alloted the old Physics Hall. This was turned into museum. Here also was created a miniature display of our excavations at Nevasa, showing the evolution of cultures from the Stone Age to the 18th century—a cultural history of no less than 2,00,000 years.

How I got the idea of doing this may be related in the following. It had been my constant desire to tell people, both educated and uneducated, the way how we archaeologists find buried things one over the other and how these finds can be visually represented in a museum. Our combined section at Nevasa, including the naturally exposed cliff on the river, and the excavated portion up to the black soil was more than 70 ft. in height. No building mediaeval or modern, is easy to come across which has this height from floor to ceiling; we have to make do with what we had. The old Deccan College buildings built in Gothic style had a ceiling 25 feet above the floor. Our task was to reduce proportionately the height of the natural and habitational layers.

The next question was who was to do this and how. I spoke to many of my colleagues and students. Then Joglekar of the Survey, an experienced photographer suggested that we should imagine one wall surface of the building as the excavated trench at Nevasa, and then show there all the characteristic objects together with the layers. Joglekar knew one A. A. Dalvi, a modeller in the Prabhat Studio at Pune. He was a past master in the art of modelling and had catered to all tastes. To him this task would not be all difficult. Moreover, being a trained modeller, he would be able to reduce all the objects to their proportionate sizes first on paper and afterwards by making models in plaster of Paris and painting them as required. Thus, a novel method of displaying a high section from excavation, spanning hundreds of thousands of years, was found out. It is now a great draw in our museum. Many foreign archaeologists— French, German, Russian, and American—have sought permissiom to photograph this, because, as I understand, few museums in the world have hit upon this method of showing the evolution of material cultures.

Later, when a new building was constructed with the University Grants Commission funds, on the opposite side as the new structure was so planned that this section could become the central theme of the museum. In this building the adjoining wall space was used for the display of maps based on the reconstruction of historical geography from the inscriptions. Museum display now-a-days is a work of art. But a museum which displays objects from several fields of archaeology is difficult to design. Antiquities go on piling up every year, and some of these have to be displayed for the immediate purpose of study by our teachers, students, and scholars. Hence, museums, like the one in the Deccan College, are essentially "study" museums where students can have a visual knowledge of the subject they are learning in their respective institutions. I consider myself fortunate that I could get such a section prepared, as also the various maps, by a team of draftsmen who made drawings of antiquities— stone tools and pottery in particular—as well as life-like reconstructions of all aspects of life, such as the potter of Navdatoli and the Navdatoli village itself some 3000 years ago. And these were done by artists who had no formal qualifications; not even a basic degree or diploma in art. And even if a qualified artist came thirty years ago I did not have the means to employ him. For except the usual Departmental grant and the *ad hoc* grant we got for research from donors and the Universities, the Deccan College had no funds for employing an artist on a permanent basis. Hence, as the need arose, funds were found out and artists were appointed on job-work basis. Perhaps in Pune alone, persons appointed on a fixed salary of Rs. 100, or so, could be found, who would work sincerely and conscientiously, often beyond office hours in the college as well as on the field. When, however, the University Grants Commission established a department and the Government of Maharashtra also sanctioned funds for permanent appointment of a photographer-draftsman, then all those artists who were appointed on job-work basis were put on permanent cadre. As a result, we did build up a very devoted team of artists. What was true of the photographer-draftsman is also true of our office staff—stenographer, clerk-cum-accountant and other employees. There was never a day when they would not turn up for work on holidays if they were asked to. It is in this spirit that we had all worked.

We ought to remember that one does not acquire knowledge for self-glorification, for writing dissertation or for getting lucrative jobs. That idea I had given up as soon as I joined the Deccan College. Thus when I was invited by Sir V. T. Krishnamachari, when he was the Dewan of Jaipur, to become the Director of Archaeology in Jaipur on a handsome salary I politely refused saying that I had prepared plans of research which could be executed only in a research institute like the Deccan College. Later, the same plea I had put before the Vice-Chancellor of the Maharaja Sayajirao University, when I was invited to go there as Professor of Archaeology on double the salary I was getting at the Deccan College. A still more tempting offer came from Calcutta with the offer of a car.

To all these invitations and others, not so expressly made, my one reply was that at the Deccan College I had unlimited scope for work which I knew I would not get elsewhere. We had built up a good library and a fairly good museum of original

122   antiquities. Above all, there was appreciation of our work as is evident from the reports of our activities and discoveries and the way scholars and laymen came to listen to our lectures which is rare in Bombay, Surat or Ahmedabad, though perhaps not at Baroda. I have always felt that in lie money and status alone are not significant. What one needs to sustain ones spirits and interest in one's work is some appreciation. That quality one still finds in Pune.

2

I have always felt that historians and archaeologists must play their part in the life of the nation. They cannot remain merely passive onlookers. They should speak out on the strength of the special knowledge they have acquired. I felt this very acutely when there were riots in Tamil Nadu, when the Government of India tried to introduce railway tickets written in Hindi only ! On the basis of historical evidence gathered from inscriptions from the third century B. C. to 1200 A.D., I pointed out how the language of the court, that is, of administration, was never the language of the masses at any period in Indian history and that it was illogical to make Hindi the only official language in India. I also pointed out that English could never be driven out from India, for it was no longer the language of the erstwhile British rulers. It had become a world language. I again reiterated the point in my convocation address to Pune University. When the speech was published in the *Times of India*, it was appreciated all over India and reproduced in other journals.

Likewise, the attempts to force the Government to stop cow-slaughter were, I thought, not right. For at no time, in the long history of India was cow-slaughter completely stopped. It could not be enforced even in a Hindu State, by king like Kumarapala who was a great patron of Jainism, and who had issued a proclamation banning slaughter of

animals but only on three days in a fortnight. This
article, though very much criticised by orthodox
people—my friends and foes—had a salutary effect.
It was later reprinted in *Seminar* with footnotes and
references.

The border riots between Maharashtrians and
Kannadigas in Belgaum and around, and the riots
in Gujarat and Madhya Pradesh pained me. If the
Maharashtrians and Kannadigas fight and burn each
other's houses, how we can teach history to our
children I wondered. Who will regard Pulakeshi
II, the Western Chalukyan King as the greatest
seventh-century king! Or who will regard Rana
Pratap or Shivaji as a national figure? On occasions
like these, we seem to forget all our history and all
our religion. In ancient India there were geographical, political and linguistic barriers. The Buddhist
bhikshus, for example, roamed throughout India
freely without having to suffer social or political
ostracism. It is this which permitted the South
Indians to go to Badri Kedar and the Gujaratis
and others to Kanyakumari and Puri. If Indian
archaeology and history teach us anything, it is the
underlying cultural unity of India which our linguistic or religious frenzy tries to destroy. Therefore, it
is our duty as historians and archaeologists to foster
this cultural unity.

Love of truth should be the guiding principle in
any branch of research and no less in history and
archaeology. Since, I love truth and propagate it, I
am very unpopular among many scholars, saints,
priests and even laymen. My study of the epics and
the Purāṇas and other traditional literature have
told me that the issues over which we often fight
are not the issues that are to be found in our epics
or the Purāṇas. These are interpolations. I had
not intended to be an iconoclast, nor am I self-
appointed critic of the century-old beliefs of our
people, but the distortions of truth I hate.

124   When my article on the cow-slaughter was published many so-called spiritual leaders and others sent
threatening letters and telegrams. I remember when
my views on the *Rāmāyana* and the *Mahābhārata*
were published by the press all over India, a lower
functionary from the National Chemical laboratory
at Pune came searching for me at the Deccan College, and asked me if what he had read about Rama
and Krishna was all wrong. How can one answer
searching questions ? I gave him what I had written
in Hindi and Marathi on these subjects. He seemed
to have been satisfied for he did not meet me since
then.

On these subjects there is certainly great scope
for telling the truth. When I wrote articles in
English or Hindi which were read by a friend in
Pune who was himself a great scholar and who knew
the *Bhāgavat Purāna* by heart and often recited the
Rāmāyana and performed *Harikirtanas*, asked me why
I had said such blasphemous things about Rama and
Sita as, for instance, Sita's pouring of one hundred
pots of wine to propitiate the river Kalindi when she
wanted to cross this mighty river at Prayag or that
in *āshrama* of Bharadwaj, at Allahabad, soldiers
of Bharata were lavishly treated with wine and
women because they refused to go either to Ayodhya
or to Chitrakuta ! He was pacified when the defini-
tive edition of the *Ayodhyā Kānda* was placed before
him. Being a good student of Sanskrit, he had little
difficulty in going through the relevant sections. He
then said, very apologetically, that he had read so
often the whole of the *Rāmāyana* but he never thought
what he was reading was repugnant to the occasion and was something interpolated. Like him there
should be many reputed scholars who have not cared
to read the whole of the *Rāmāyana* critically.

3

Those reading my autobiography might be
curious to know what in my opinion is the future of

Indian Archaeology. If the truth is to be told
without any embellishment, since I have watched the
activities of the archaeologists at close quarters in
several states and universities as also in the Archaeological Survey of India, I must say that the future
of archaeology in India is very bleak indeed !
Through the centuries in India the purse string of
knowledge has been held first by the Kshatriya
oligrachy and then later by the Brahmin clerics.
Later when the heads of the states, the *jāgīrdārs*
and *zamīndārs*, came to power the lower echelons in
the departments and in the Archaeological Survey
of India as well as the teachers in the universities,
barring a few exceptions, have had little freedom to
plan and execute their plans of studies. Almost all
of them are expected to carry out the work assigned
by the so-called "head". It is this person—the
headless "head" —who arrogates to himself all knowledge and hence all power. Unless he approved no
report could be published. Very often without doing
any work and just because he has happened to secure
the grant and permission for the exploration, or excavation the head would insist that his name must be
associated with the actual work. He sees to it that his
name is mentioned first and often the head omits the
names of his colleagues who have been working for
years and who may have done all the work but are
gracious enough and do not mind if their names are
mentioned in the footnote. But many protest.

The result is that almost everywhere numerous,
small and big, reports of excavations or explorations
lie unpublished, while there are cases when reports
have not been prepared at all. One Head, because
he could not get the report prepared, had the teme-
rity to tell me that the assistants who helped him to
excavate, lack training in the art of writting reports.
How does one get training except by writing? Whether in a university or in a state department, the
Head must, particularly if he is himself not qualified
to write the report, allow his assistants to do this
work, and get it published in the name of his assis-

126 tant. Unfortunately this has become a matter of prestige. The Head is supposed to be omniscient. He alone can write a report, though in practice, all the donkey work at various levels is done by his assistants. The Head merely puts his signature or at best summarises the contents of the report.

The practice began with Sir Mortimer Wheeler. But it had some justification in Wheeler's case while there is none in the case of his successors who are hardly fit to hold the candle. But they proudly strut about declaring that such-and-such work was done under their direction and that so-and-so had contributed this-or-that account. I had to fight against this pernicious practice for the last twenty-five years. Two years ago when I could not bear this any longer, I had to say in an open meeting of the Central Advisory Board of Archaeology that the *zamindari* system in archaeology must be abolished lock, stock and barrel. There was a hue and cry. I was told that some heads rushed to the chairman (minister) and told him that I should not have been allowed to say what I had said. Fortunately there was no emergency at that time, otherwise they would have thrown me in jail.

What I have said makes unpleasant reading. But I am destined to speak the truth even if it is unpleasant. Unless a person like Wheeler—who is born once in a century—once again brings fresh air blow into our universities, state deparments of archaeology and in the Archaeological Survey of India, the future of archaeology in India is bleak. Or else, the authorities will have to take a broom and blow away the cobwebs from the brains of these August bodies. They have to do what they have done for bonded labour and farmers and others who for centuries were under the clutches of the money-lenders. If freedom is given there will be no frustr-ation and the teacher in a university or an assistant in an Archaeology Department will have the incen-tive to do original work and, above all, try and

experiment on new concepts in archaeology. Archaeolgy has to be reborn in India.

When the history of archaeology, anthropology, sociology and linguistics comes to be written in India it will be said that what my colleague Dr Karve and Dr Katre and I did could not be done because we had plenty of freedom to plan and execute at the Deccan College, though our means for nearly twenty years were very slender. The freedom that we enjoyed, we shared with our assistants and students, thus allowing them to develop according to their capacities. Thus each one of my pupils who joined me as an assistant first, and then became a lecturer, has now made a name in his own field of specialisation in India and abroad. As long as the spirit of freedom prevails an institution will continue to grow.

Though the future of archaeology appears to be bleak, a way must be found, and things will surely improve if the changes that I have been envisaging since 1964 are introduced. As a member of the Wheeler Committee, I had suggested that the functions of the Archaeological Survey should be clearly defined. One wing should look after conservation or preservation of monuments; the other wing should devote itself to research. At present both these functions are so much mixed up that research —excavation and exploration—and, particularly, the writing of the reports are neglected.

Not less than twenty-five big and small reports on the work done since 1960 are still pending publication. I cannot blame the officers of the Survey. Two things come in their way: First, though an officer might have done an excellent excavation, say at Kalibangan, or carried out a very promising exploration, say in Rajasthan, routine office work does not allow him to prepare the report. This is primarily because conservation is thought to be the all-and-end-all of the Archaeological Survey of India.

Secondly, the transfer of the officials. An officer may have done an excellent piece of work on the site but since he has to be transferred or promoted he has to abandon the excavation or exploration of that site. This is how with numerous projects undertaken by the officers all over India were nipped in the bud. While the Archaeological Survey of India is doing an excellent job in the domain of conservation, the same cannot be said about excavation.

Some of my pupils, after they joined the Archaeological Survey of India, were burdened with so much routine work that no time was left for research. And if this happens year after year then even the best scholar in the world will rot.

Likewise, if the universities wish to undertake excavations and explorations as the Deccan College has been doing since 1939, then they have to have two cotegories of teachers: teachers who will do teaching at the under-graduate and post-graduate level, and teachers who will do some teaching at the post-graduate level but their main job must be confined to regional surveys and small and large-scale excavations.

It is in this way alone that the sites like Kausambi could be properly excavated by the Allahabad University or Hastinapur by the Kurukshetra University and similar sites in Bihar by the Patna University. Both Baroda and Nagpur Universities have followed the example set by Pune and they have published reports whatever explorations or excavations they have done in the course of the last two decades. The Universities in Andhra, Karnataka and Tamil Nadu have to follow the same plan.

Thus there is hope. If these suggestions which are based on my experience of the last thirty-seven years are implemented, if fundamental changes are effected in the working of the Archaeological Survey of India and in the departments of archaeology in

the various states and universities, and if freedom of
action in planning, excavation and writing is given
there is no reason why the members of the staff cannot achieve a great deal in the actual work of exploration and excavation.

No longer should the head—whether he is the
Director-General of Archaeology or the Director of
Explorations, Excavations or a State Director of
Archaeology or the head of a University or a professor of Eminence—arrogate to himself the credit due
to his assistants. Such freedom alone can dispel the
present gloom of frustration which prevails in archaeological departments throughout India.

As for the future plan of work at the Deccan
College, I may say here a few words. It should be
clear from my account how the various branches of
historical archaeology in which I was interested,
came to be developed. Prehistory or proto-history
was initiated because it was so willed, not because
I had thought of it. These departments in the
Deccan College are working fairly well, each one
discharging his duty of teaching and conducting
research work to the best of his ability in his own
specific line of specialization. Just as each federat-
ing unit or state in a federal republic goes on doing its
routine work, thereby contributing to the health and
wealth of the centre, in the same way at the Deccan
College for the solution of complex problems, such as
settlement patterns of the Neolithic and Megalithic
cultures in South India, it will be necessary for each
sub-department not only to contribute its expert
knowledge, but even its funds, if large funds are
scarce or are not available. It must not be forgotten
that at present the Deccan College is the only institute which is working according to a plan and if
some large, national and international problems are
to be solved then each department of the college is
expected to do its bit. I made this suggestion while
I was the head of a department of the Deccan
College and I put the suggestion in writing because

some members wanted me to indicate the future line of work. However, I have no desire to tie the hands of the present head or any future head and I must leave the things as they are—*jase asel tase*, as Sri Upasani Baba has taught me.

4

I have discussed elsewhere that some fifteen years ago, scholars, particularly young Americans, have been talking of New Archaeology, doubting the wisdom and methods of the veterans of the earlier generation. As usual, some of our young scholars were caught by this blizzard of controversy and attacked some of us in a similar way. In order therefore, to learn their, particularly the American, point of view, I decided to acquaint myself with their aims and methods. I found to my surprise that some of those I had already anticipated in 40's when I was working on the temples of Gujarat and collecting blades and other implements from Navdatoli. But an American student who was at the Deccan College told me that I had not conceptualized these methods and aims. This may be so. But I have always found from my experience that, what is essential, is the mastery over one's material whether it be stone tools or temples and once you have masterd your facts you know how best to interpret the available data. Unfortunately, the fashion today is to avoid the first and concentrate on the second leading one to making gross errors of interpretations of the artifacts.

As far as the other aims and goals of new Archaeology are concerned, after a careful study of these so-called more advanced methods, I have pointed out in my D.N. Majumdar lectures on "New Archaeology, Its Scope and Application in India" and to what extent we can adopt these. The adoption of these aims and methods requires more hard and exacting work in the field. This unfortunately our young and old scholars are not prepared to do. As

for the Americans, I must say that all their "fads"
and theories are preceded and followed by most
painstaking and exacting work.

5

"Have I been successful in finding where the
Aryans had settled in India?" Though a straight-
forward answer cannot be given, we now know
where to look for them. Bal Gangadhar Tilak saw
them in the North Pole, Sir Mortimer Wheeler
found them at Harappa and Mohenjodaro, Prof.
Lal thought they had settled at Hastinapur, and I
discovered them at Navdatoli. The Aryans are
always playing hide-and-seek game with us. But the
game has to go on for sometime to come.

As these last lines are being written, I came
across an article in the *Readers Digest* of October
1976, about the benefits of meditation by Dr Herbert
Benson. Dr Benson is an Associate Professor of medicine at the Harvard Medical School, and Director
of the hypertension section of Boston's Beth Israel
Hospital. I had previously read some of the important articles on Maharshi Mahesh's transcendental
meditation and had also undergone a brief course of
training. Scientific tests have proved that even
twenty minutes of meditation, twice a day, by repea-
ting the word *Om* would calm ones nerves and
reduce blood-pressure. However, the effect of this
practice will last as long as one continues it.

But it is often forgotten that if one continues to
meditate for a few months, then very probably it
will become a part of his life. Moreover, if such a
meditation, which is purely and solely undertaken
for physiological needs, is directed towards spiritual
ends, as the Indians were told to do from time
immemorial, one can well visualize the benefits of
this meditation for oneself and the world. It is this
aspect that the seers in India and elsewhere have
been emphasising over and over again. In fact, if

we give a spiritual or divine direction to the actions in life, then certainly a greater and truer equality will prevail in the world. That will be real communism or socialism.

It is often asked how I could guide so many students and write on so many varied subjects. The explanation is very simple. There was always a desire to learn something new which interested me, and also simultaneously a desire to share that new knowledge, however significant or insignificant, important or unimportant it may be, with others. For I have instinctively felt that knowledge is like a flame; you light it and it spreads; conceal it and it dies. Of course, this has one draw-back, and that is, I cannot keep any knowledge secret which is the custom with some scholars, and particularly with the heads of the Archaeological Survey of India. Of course, this tendency to acquire and share knowledge with others is not common even among my own pupils and colleagues. I remember many occasions when I had to coax or scold some pupils because they would hold back some information which they possessed. We all forget why Dattatreya is worshipped today, and particularly on Thursdays, because he was always keen on learning even from the meanest and the lowest like ants and prostitutes in order to pass that knowledge to others. This has been beautifully described in the eleventh *skandha* of the *Bhāgavata Purāṇa*. It tells us that before one becomes a good teacher, one must be a good pupil.

With regard to teaching and guiding my pupils, I have always taken into consideration their background—social, financial and educational—in details of each pupil who came to me for guidance. No pupil was asked to work on a subject on which I had personally not worked or thought or written. There was no leap in the dark, as is often the case with many guides who without any personal experience of the subject simply leave the students to their fate. Two instances of such callousness I should like to relate.

By 1950 the [Deccan College had acquired a reputation as a centre of prehistoric research. Hence students were sent here from various universities in India for training. At that time Sir Mortimer Wheeler had just left India. He had severely criticized the unplanned work in Indian archaeology since its inception and particularly after 1924. He had, therefore, emphasised the need of problem-oriented archaeology.

The word 'problem' was then very much in the air. I must cite an instance. A Professor, who had little experience of research in prehistory, gave one of his first Ph.D. students the problem of microliths and that is because the student or the teacher's assistant had collected exactly 100 microliths. He was therefore supposed to write a thesis on these. The student remained at the Deccan College for more than six months. During this period we made him acquire the necessary background, and asked him to participate in our prehistoric expeditions. The poor student did all this at his own expense and I was glad that he was a sincere student. Not only was he prepared to undergo all kinds of hardship, but was also intelligent. So, after his training, he realised that the problem of his 100 microliths could not be solved simply by classifying and re-classifying and making drawings of these microliths !

These microliths had to be put in their space-time context. To do this he must excavate—even in a small way—some sites, where these microliths were picked up exactly as we had done in Gujarat in 1941. Unfortunately, neither his teacher nor the university would help him financially as the Deccan College had been doing, since it became necessary in India, unlike Wheeler's method in England, for the students to pay for their boarding and lodging while on an excavation tour. Luckily, the student belonged to a good middle-class family, and his father had no objection to his spending Rs. 1.000 or so on a small excavation. After completing the excavation this student came once more to the Deccan College, this time to write out the thesis. Since he was not registered at Pune University, but elsewhere, he submitted the thesis for the Ph.D. degree to that university.

The matter did not end here. The university asked me to evaluate the thesis as an external referee and also to take his viva. Both were wrong, and undesirable steps but a greater shock was in store for me. Just when I was about to ask the student to explain the stratification, the teacher apologetically told me that he had not checked the stratification in the field. At least this much was expected of the teacher since the site of the excavation was not more than one hundred miles away from his university. Since I knew the student well enough having seen his work in the field and also in the laboratory, I had no hesitation in declaring him fit for the Ph.D. Later, the teacher became an 'expert' in prehistory and got his promotion.

While I was indeed glad that a new centre of prehistoric research was coming up, I was sorry the way the things were managed. So the next time when this trick was repeated elsewhere, I had to put my foot down, and brought it to the notice of the U.G.C. In this case the interesting thing was that the student "defected". He refused to go back to the university from where he had come. But he had paid the fees and filled up its terms in that university. So in his own interest I advised him to submit the thesis to that university. Fortunately the Vice-Chancellor appreciated my point of view, and much against the rules of the university nominated me the internal referee and appointed a panel of external referees to adjudicate on the thesis.

Both these incidents, which started as "small problems", are actually symptoms, of deep malice from which the universities are suffering today. It

is next to impossible that the U.G.C. or any other government agency can completely rid the universities of these foul practices. But some improvement might take place, if some norms are strictly and impartially implemented irrespective of the position or status of the teacher. We have just now heard how a British scientist manipulated results of his experiments and misled the entire scientific world. Of course, some of my younger colleagues did not like or appreciate my views of sharing of knowledge. They are of the opinion that what we learn by way of excavation or exploration is meant for personal aggrandizement.

In 1961-62, we dug at Ahar, close to Udaipur. Here particularly the house-plans that were found were identical with those which are still found on the foot of the excavated mound of Dhūlkoṭa in the village of Pala. This village is predominantly of the Bhils. Naturally the presumption would be that probably the early settlers of Ahar, some 4,000 years ago, were not Aryans or some foreigners but the aborginal autochthons. However, this presumption can be proved or discarded only if a proper, systematic ethnographic study of the Bhils at Pala and in the vicinity of Ahar is carried out. And for such a study we must have students preferably with specialisation in anthropology. After Malati Nagar had completed her anthropological study, she wanted naturally to compare her results with the archaeological finds. Those were still being studied and not fully published. And the problem was, as is always the case in Indian universities and in the Archaeological Survey of India : "How can the unpublished material be utilized by persons other than those who participated in the excavations ?"

On this and similar questions I have always taken a very liberal view. Here Wheeler's example inspired me. He had sent me pieces of glass bangles found by him in Taxila excavations for my study of the antiquity of glass bangles in India. So I thought that there was nothing wrong if Malati Nagar utilised our material. For such a study alone would help us to know who the Aharians were. One cannot get to know it merely by describing the pottery.

6

There were a few occasions in my life which made me protest against authority, even against the highest in the land to see that justice was done. In almost all cases success has crowned my efforts. The first is the case of Dr Vale. He was one of our students in linguistics. After getting his Ph.D., he had joined the Education Department of Bombay State. One day, sometime in 1953-54, I met him on the Lloyd Bridge in Pune. Seeing him downcast and sullen I enquired as to what had happened and why he was looking so worried. He told me briefly that he was without a job. I asked him to see me at the Deccan College.

The case of Dr Vale is typical of all government departments. He was an education inspector and posted in Baroda in the Old Bombay State. For some reason he was suspended and enquiries were made against him. Though a year or two passed and the enquiry did not reveal anything against him, the suspension continued. As if this was not enough the education department issued orders that Dr Vale should not be employed by any educational institution. The whole thing appeared to me fishy and most unjust. I, therefore, asked Vale to bring his file to me. I studied the case, and found that the government were completely unjustified in suspending him and issuing the orders as they had done.

I asked Dr Katre if Vale could not be given some post in the dictionary department at our college. He was willing, but the then Director of Educa-ion, Dr Bhandarkar, objected saying that Dr Vale should first withdraw the case against the government. This Vale would certainly do provided the government withdrew the unjust restrictions against his re-employment. This was done, and Dr Vale joined our Dictionary Department and retired only a few years ago.

Dr S.N. Ojha's case was of a slightly different nature. For the last twenty-five years or so Ojha had been serving as a lecturer in Gujarati, and in 1970 he applied for the position of the senior lecturership in the Ferguson College. Seniority in a college or the university is governed by certain rules and procedures. The university accordingly had appointed, what was then called, the Placement Committee to which committee the principal of each college had to send his recommendations. Though Dr Ojha's seniority was established, for some reason, the Ferguson College did not give him the senior grade. I therefore, represented the matter to the Pune University as a member of the Executive Council. In spite of several meetings with the principal, who was also a member of the Executive Council, nothing happened. Ultimately in protest I tendered my resignation to the Chancellor (Governor) from the membership of the Executive Committee. Thereupon the Executive Council once again considered Dr Ojha's case, and finally directed the Ferguson College authorities to implement its decision. Of course, by getting the senior grade Dr Ojha did not gain financially but had the satisfaction of seeing that justice had been done to him. But the matter did not rest there. *Kesari*, the famous Marathi newspaper in Pune, tried to represent the case of Dr Ojha's apponents to which a reply had to be given by me through its columns. In both these cases, I did not suffer personally, though the newspaper controversy projected my personality, in a different capacity.

So far, I was known only as an archaeologist. Now I was taken to be a zealot. Another incident brought me directly in conflict with the Vice-Chance-

138   llor. According to the rules of the Deccan College, the Vice-Chancellor of the Pune University is also the Chairman of the Council of Management of the Deccan College, the director of the college occupying a lower position.

It so happened that when Dr B.P. Apte became the Vice-Chancellor, he appointed one of the Executive Council members, who then happened to be his fast friend as the liaison officer between the Deccan College and the University. This gentleman borrowed a number of books from the Deccan College library. When he did not return the books, the Librarian was in a fix. Ultimately, he sent a reminder. This displeased the Vice-Chancellor, who immediately sent for the Director, Dr Katre, and the Librarian, Shri Belsare on some pretext. Calling the latter inside his chamber, he scolded, the Librarian for his impudent action. Poor Belsare came out of the room completely downcast. Throughout his twenty years of service as the Librarian he never had such an experience. He related to me the entire episode when I rejoined my post as the Joint Director after the termination of the Nehru Fellowship.

Belsare's story so much upset me that for a moment I could not decide what steps to take against the erosion of 'our independence'. Ultimately I wrote to the Vice-Chancellor that when the Librarian had sent the reminder to his friend, he had just done his duty. I wrote to him saying that he had once sent even a second reminder to the Chancellor who was the Governor because it was the duty of the Librarian to do so. He should not, therefore, regard this reminder as a personal insult. Had we not taken this step we would have failed in our duty. He should, therefore, advise his friend to return the books and we would be glad to lend him again the same books when required. The books were thus returned and the matter ended there.

However, I had to fight against the same Vice-

Chancellor when he said that the advance to the
Centre in Archaeology given by the University
Grants Commission was given to the university, and
not to the Deccan College. I pointed out to him
politely that the report of the Expert Committee
had clearly mentioned that this assistance was to be
given to the Deccan College, because during the last
twenty years or so it was the Deccan College which
had been doing work on prehistory and proto-history.
When the Vice-Chancellor persisted in his interpretation, I had to approach the U.G.C. to clarify their
position. After a full and fresh consideration they
reaffirmed their earlier decision.

I must say here emphatically that the decision
was taken by the U.G.C. on the merit of the case.
I had not met any member or the secretary of the
U.G.C. to canvass our case. I mention this because
there were some people, even at the Deccan College,
who thought that I had brought pressure on some
members of the U.G.C. This is not my habit nor
is it in my nature. Neither for Dr Vale nor for Dr
Ojha I had approached any body in the government,
or any member of the Executive Council.

I had not approached anyone even when there
was a threat of physical injury on my person. The
occasion for this was sapparently a very small incident.

Since 1963 we have been staying in a house built
by me on the campus of the Deccan College called
"Satchidananda". To the west and south-west of our
house the entire area was occupied by the military.
Now there are a few buildings here but before 1972
there was none. Occasionally a few tents would be
put up. In this no man's land a milkman had built
a hut. Then one day in the month of February-
March, the military put up a barbed wire fence
around this area. While doing so they left no opening for the milkman to go in or come out. When I
returned from the college in the evening, the milkman
who was standing outside this fence, was pleading

with the sentry to allow him to get inside the fence
to have his cup of tea which his wife had prepared.
The scene was pitious. I wrote immediately to the
military authorities that what they had done was
neither just nor right. They should have left a
passage for the milkman's family or if they did not
want him to stay there he should have been legally
evicted. No reply was received. Then on the
Hanuman Jayanti Day at about 11 p.m., all of a
sudden, we heard the sound of bomb-like crackers,
and the jawans running about in the field. This did
not stop but was repeated again at 1 a.m. and 4 a.m.
My wife and I and the inmates of the ladie's hostel
which is adjacent to this plot thought that the
jawans were celebrating the Hanuman Jayanti! But
no, these bomb explosions continued day after day
and then it soon dawned upon us that the command-
ing officer was deliberately getting this done with a
view to harrassing me and all the neighbours. One
day, their officer came to see me in my house with
his orderly. He threatened me for interfering in
their affairs. I told him that the military had enor-
mous resources, and if they chose they could easily
put up a hut for the milkman and his family somewhere nearby.

Though the officer initially talked rather haughti-
ly, he appreciated my point of view and left. The
matter did not rest there. At night my bedroom
window overlooking the Deccan College Road was
stoned and the glasspane broken. From that time
we had to keep the window closed. The person-
in-charge of this area was so much enraged that
when we were away for a week at Sakori, the military tried to close my usual entrance by putting up
a barbed wire fence. They had no right to do so
because it was a public road.

All these left a bad taste in my mouth and I felt
that the military everywhere whether in Germany,
England, Pakistan, America or India are blind to
reason. Might is right is their philosophy of action.

Night-bombing continued for a month-and-a-half but I did not protest except writing to the Police Commissioner for the daily nuisance that was caused to me and the entire neighbourhood. But he seemed to be helpless, as the culprits were military officers.

Then a friend reported the matter to Jayantrao Tilak, a member of the Rajya Sabha from Pune. And Tilak conveyed the information to Sardar Swaran Singh, who was then the Defence Minister. When he inquired into the matter he was informed by the local officer that some urgent military manoeuvres were being conducted, and these would stop only at the end of the month! While all the earlier incidents had not caused much physical and mental anguish to me or to my wife, the encounter with military had been very trying, because for more than a month we could not sleep peacefully.

I was made to take still more serious step during the Emergency. In June 1976, the son of a very close relative and friend of mine was arrested and taken to the Amaravati Jail. A well-known cardiologist, he was attached to the St. Georges Hospital. It was alleged that he was in league with a smuggler who was kept for some time in the hospital. This was a rude shock to the old parents and his young wife and children. When I learnt about this I went to see the family at Santa Cruz in Bombay. At that time they were all trying to get their son released through the intercession of friends who had once held very high position in the government.

I told them before leaving that the only thing I could do was to write to the Prime Minister, Indira Gandhi. I had never met her personally but I found her very courteous, because whenever I wrote, within days I would receive an acknowledgement or a reply. This was rarely the case with the other dignitories, except the late Governor of Maharashtra, Shri Ali Yavar Jung. He too replied to my

142   letters promptly and showed a keen interest in my
work.

So, when my friend's efforts failed, I volunteered
to write to the Prime Minister. I had written to
her thrice. Though some personal risk was involved in this, I thought that this was the least that I
could do as an educationist and a culture-historian for
a cause that was surely just. I wrote to the Prime
Minister in one of the letters, that even in olden
times when kings like Aurangzeb reigned with abso-
lute power, any aggrieved person once a month could
approach the Emperor in the open durbar. During
the Emergency, I wrote, she had left no way at all
to exercise one's elementary human right. When I
wrote this I was told that my letter might not be
appreciated, and that I might be clapped in jail.

Meanwhile elections were declared and the
Emergency was relaxed. So my friend, in fact a
cousin, thought that if he approached the Chief
Minister he could now intervene and get his son
released. So he again wrote to me on March 16
to write to the Prime Minister. This time, however, both my wife and I thought that it was no use
writing to her and I quoted the famous verse from
Kalidasa's *Reghuvaṁśa: Yāñcā meghā varmadhigune
nādhame labdhakāmāḥ* meaning, it is better to have
our wishes remain unfulfilled by good persons than
to have them fulfilled by bad ones.

I asked my friend to wait until March 24. And
then, as the world knows, a new page in history was
written. The Emergency was lifted, and my nephew
and thousands of others like him, all innocent souls,
were released.

7

I might also mention the small part that I played
in the compilation of the Dictionary of Sanskrit on
Historical Principles. This dictionary, unique of its

kind, and the largest, if completed even in 100
years, was started originally by Dr Katre with the
nucleus of the staff of the Department of Linguistics
in the Deccan College. Subsequently it was
taken over by the Government of India and regular
grants followed every year. Grants were also made
available by some universities and the UNESCO.
Further help came when the University Grants
Commission opened an advanced centre of linguistics in the Pune University which was located at the
Deccan College. Thus, since its inception in about
1947-48 until Dr Katre retired in 1970, the Dictionary Project was going on with the financial help
from several quarters.

But when Dr Katre retired, and later went over
to the United States, and some of the sources stopped
giving financial help there were doubts if the projcct
could continue. The Government help was most
vital. Naturally, the staff was very much worried,
because if the Dictionary Project stopped then they
would be without employment.

The most important decision I had to take as the
Director of the Institute was about the continuance
of the Project. I called a meeting of the department
and assured its members that under no circumstances
should the project be discontinued, though I could
not guarantee employment to all the members. In
archaeology, as in linguistics, the Deccan College
had gained international recognition and in the latter
field, it was due primarily to the Dictionary Project.
So this Project, I thought, could not be given up as
some of our critics desired. My critics even went to
the length of saying that there were no scholars in
India who could handle the project and so it must
be dropped. This was a gteat slur on Indian scholarship, particularly after a century and more of Sans-
kritic studies and specially when in Pune and Baroda,
our scholars had completed the gigantic task of
compiling the critical editions of the *Mahabharata*
and the *Ramayana*.

144   Though I knew that the preparation of the proposed dictionary required scholarship and an entirely
different nature of set-up, I felt that given devotion,
dedication and determination the editing work of the
dictionary could continue and a couple of volumes
could be published in our life-time.

These qualities Dr Ghatge possessed in no small
measure. Hence I had recommended his name to
Dr Katre when the problem of a Joint-Director had
arisen a second time. I had told him that if any
one was likely to discharge the responsibility of
editing the dictionary, it was he. This suggestion
displeased some members of the Deccan College,
but I am glad to say that my dream was partially
fulfilled after ten years when the late President
Fakhruddin Ali Ahmed released the first facsimile of
the dictionary. The Second was released by the
Prime Minister Shri Morarji Desai. Though it
would be foolish to expect the completion of the
gigantic project in this century, there is the hope
and satisfaction that on the foundation so well laid,
our successors at the Deccan College would find the
means to raise the infrastructure, if they show the
same spirit as Dr Katre and Dr Ghatge did.

I should also like to add that with the division
of the Archaeological Survey of India into Research
and Conservation, one may expect that the two
departments might help the growth of scientific
archaeology in a planned manner. Here again we
must have some devoted and dedicated persons ;
otherwise such organisations can achieve very little.
The Archaeological Society of India of which I
happen to be the chairman since its inception has
had several annual meetings and very fruitful discussions, particularly at Varanasi, Nagpur, Kurukshetra
Chandigarh and Jaipur. The Prehistoric Society
which was founded only four years ago has now en-
larged its scope of activity and has changed its name
into Indian Society for Prehistoric and Quaternary
Studies. This is welcome. And it is hoped that it

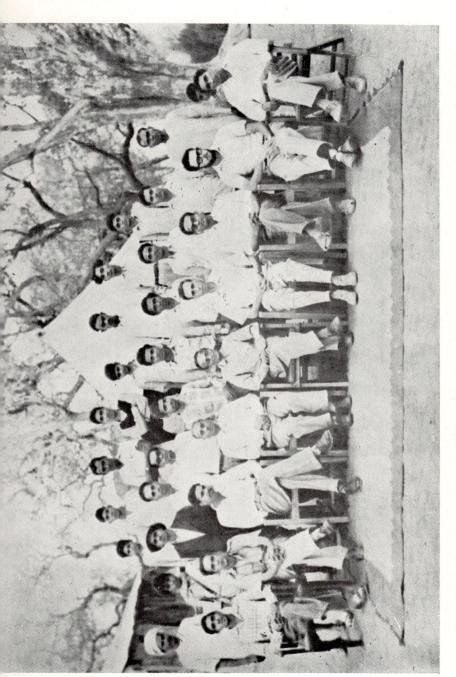

Prof. Sankalia with students, colleagues and members of the staff, Indian as well as foreign, at Navdatoli excavations Camp, 1957-58.

Prof. Gadgil's wife, his wife, colleagues and members of the staff at Hingne

Reconstruction of the excavated levels at Nevasa, Maharashtra, exhibited in the Central Hall of the Museum of the Deccan College, Pune.

Prof. Sankalia with Prof. R.C. Majumdar and others at the Tripuri Camp, 1967.

Prof. Sankalia with Mrs. and Mr. Genscher, Minister for Interior, Federal Govt. of Germany, at the opening of a wing of Indian Art in the Museum of Oriental Art, Berlin-1971.

Prof. Sankalia with Sir Mortimer Wheeler on the dining table
in a Seminar held at Patna. Prof. Sankalia is showing
a laboratory-produced black-and-red ware bowl to
Dr. Wheeler

Prof. Sankalia with Prof. F. E. Zeuner during an
explorationtrip on the Sabarmati-1949

Honour of the City being conferred on Prof. Sankalia by the Chairman of the Ahmadnagar Municipality, 1973.

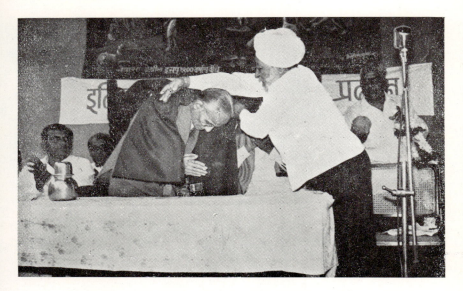

Prof. Sankalia receiving the Gold Medal from Gujarat
Sahitya Sabha, Ahmedabad, 1967.

President V. V. Giri conferring the title of Padma Bhushan
on Prof. Sankalia, 1974.

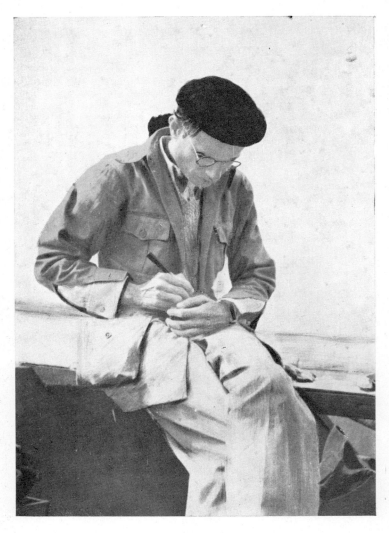

Prof. Sankalia, the explorer.　On the Narmada
at Maheshwar, 1957-58.

will very soon justify its new name. The former **145**
Society publishes *Paratattva*, an annual bulletin,
while the latter Society publishes *Man and Environment*, again an annual bulletin.

With regard to the journals, which these Societies
are publishing, I am frankly not happy. India is a
poor country and an academic journal does not have
many subscribers. Under the circumstances it is
certainly difficult to run a journal, whether it be a
quarterly or a six monthly or an annual publication.
Besides we have also a dearth of good writers and
discerning editors. Most of the editors are merely
collectors. There are very few editors who have
the time, energy and capacity for editing. And if
any editor blue pencils the writer, it has often
been reported, feels offended. Hence the normal
practice is to send the articles straight to the
press.

We shall have a journal of international standard
when the following four conditions are julfilled :
1. The articles for at least three consecutive
numbers must be collected in advance; 2. Irrespective
of the personality of the writer, the articles must be
published after the Editor has carefully gone through
them; 3. competent and dedicated editors must be
found out; and 4. there should be sufficient funds
for publication. Unless these conditions are fulfilled,
it is no use having a number of journals. Very often
these journals live for a short time and die a premature death.

Before I close I have to relate a very unfortunate
event at the Deccan College. I had thought that
though intrigues and infighting had become a
common feature in our academic life all over India
today, it was absent in my department. Very often I
had chosen this or that person to fill up a particular
post, after that person, though not necessarily brilliant, had shown some aptitude and promise so that
a particular line which I wanted to develop at the

146   Deccan College could be developed.

The question of 'succession' had also been easily settled. However, a thing that I had feared when I became the Director began to take an unpleasant (ugly) shape. Owing to purely historical reasons, we have two separate departments of archaeology. One, the older one, belongs to this Deccan College; and the other was started by the University, after it was founded in 1948. Both are located at the Deccan College, in a building, which belongs to the University, but on a land which is owned by the Deccan College.

For a long time I looked after both the departments. But according to the University regulation, the Head of a University Department can be a Reader or a Professor appointed by the University. Thus I ceased to be the Head of the University Department, and one of my very young pupils who was appointed a Reader, became the Head. However, since both the departments had been developed by me, and were manned by my pupils, nothing untoward happened, though, in fact, legally there were two separate departments.

This dyarchy was undesirable, I knew. And I had often tried to get it abolished, and I nearly succeeded when the Government itself had issued a G.R. to that effect that the University Department of Archaeology and Linguistics be merged with those of the Deccan College. Unfortunately, a few students of the Old Deccan College did not like this move and got the merger stayed.

Meanwhile, I retired in 1973. The person who succeeded me felt this difference acutely because there were two distinct authorities. Naturally, like myself, he could not exercise *de facto* authority over both the departments, though in age and experience, he was the senior of the two. More undesirable consequences of 'mine' and 'thine' occured. I tried to intervene once or twice but without much effect.

But when the University, under the U.G.C. development plan, decided to have a Professorship in archaeology the matters came to a head. Though by discussing with the U.G.C. Committee, it was decided to have a Professorship in prehistoric archaeology, the University decided to have a Professor either in prehistory or historic archaeology.

The University asked me to lay down qualifications for both the posts and also suggest a panel of experts. This I did. What happened afterwards I do not have first-hand knowledge. For some reasons, the panels which I had prepared were not placed before the Executive Council. The panel which was prepared later was heavily loaded in favour of the non-university candidates. Of the three experts, only one had some general acquaintance with prehistory, the other two were students of historic archaeology and not competent to sit on judgement for such an important post.

Obviously, there was an attempt to rig the panel, so much so that when one of the experts arrived, and set his foot on the railway platform he was literally whisked away, least he should meet any other person (like myself). The interview was indeed nominal.

When I saw all these things happening before my own eyes, I literally wept, not because the Department, which had been developed from nothing, was being torn into pieces, but because for exercising authority all the worst aspects of human nature had gained ascendency. I realized, as I had never realized before, that of all the bad aspects of human nature—*kama, krodha, mada* and *ahankara*—the last two were the worst. Hence Shri Upasani Baba had repeatedly advised his followers to subdue feeling of 'I' and to always accept an humble position.

148   As I write the last line of this autobiography, I look back with wonder and think of the seers who had written the *samhitas* long ago and so correctly predicted about my interest in archaeology and the recognition that I would get. According to them, I was born to be an archaeologist. And I did become one. What sort of powers did these seers have to peer into the future ?

Author's Bio-data and Books

BIO-DATA OF DR H.D. SANKALIA

Professor Emeritus, Deccan College, Pune 411 006.

1. **Name :** HASMUKH DHIRAJLAL SANKALIA

2. **Date of Birth : 10-12-1908, Bombay**

3. **Academic Carrer :**

   > M. A. Ist Class in Ancient Indian History, Bombay University, 1932.
   > LL. B. Bombay University, 1931.
   > Ph. D. Archaeology, London University, 1937.

4. **Positions held :**

   (*a*) Professor of Proto-Indian and Ancient Indian History, and Head of the Department of History, Deccan College, 1939-73.

   (*b*)   (*i*) Director (Acting) Deccan College 1956-59.
   (*ii*) Jt. Director, Deccan College 1960-68.
   (*iii*) Director, Deccan College, 1970-73 (Dec.).

   (*c*) Professor-in-charge of the Department of Archaeology, University of Poona, 1948-68 and later.

   (*d*) University Grants Commission Teacher 1974-76.

5. **Present Position :**

   (*a*) Professor Emeritus in Archaeology, Deccan College (since 11th December 1973—   )

   (*b*) Hon. Director, Tilak Maharashtra Vidyapeeth, Poona, (since August 1975—   )

a. **Awards :**

   (*a*) Prizes

152

   (*b*) Fellowships
   (*c*) Honorary Fellowships
   (*d*) Public Honours.

(a) *Prizes :*

  (*i*) Bhagwanlal Indraji Prize, Bombay University, 1933.
  (*ii*) Silver Medal, Royal Asiatic Society, Bombay, 1944.
  (*iii*) Gold Medal, Gujarat Sahitya Sabha, Ahmedabad, 1967.
  (*iv*) Dadabhoy Naoroji Prize for 1968, Bombay.
  (*v*) The Chakrabarty Silver Medal, Asiatic Society, Bengal, Calcutta, 1972.
  (*vi*) The Robert Bruce Foote Plaque, Department of Anthropology, University of Calcutta, Calcutta, 1974.
  (*vii*) Om Hari Prize, South Gujarat University, Surat 1975.
  (*viii*) The Campbell Memorial Gold Medal for 1974, Asiatic Society, Bombay 1977.
  (*ix*) Prize of Rs. 1,000/- Govt. of India for the Marathi Book on Introduction to Archaeology, 1971.
  (*x*) Prize of Rs. 1,000/-, Gujarat Govt. for the book in Gujarati on Archaeology and the Ramayana, 1976.

(b) *Fellowship :* Jawaharlal Nehru Fellowship 1968-70.

(c) *Honorary Fellowships & Memberships.*

  (*i*) All India Sanskrit Academy, Lucknow, 1974.
  (*ii*) Ethnographic and Folklore Society of UP, Lucknow 1974.
  (*iii*) Haras Institute, St. Xavier's College, Bombay 1977.
  (*iv*) Honorary Member, Indo-Pacific Prehistory Association, Canberra, Australia, 1976.
  (*v*) Indian Society for Pre-historic and Studies (ISPAS) India, 1977.

(d) *Public Honours :*

  (*i*) *Manɛpatra.* by the citizens of Maheshwar, Madhya Bharat State, 1954 (for excavations at Maheshvar and Navdatoli).
  (*ii*) Manapatra and Shawl, by the Ahmednagar Municipality, Ahmed-

nagar 1973 (for bringing to light the history of Ahmednagar District from the dim part—by excavations and explorations at and around Nevasa.

(*iii*) Manapatra and Shawl, by

Poona Municipal Corporation, Poona 1974.

(*iv*) Padma Bhushan for distinguished work in Prehistory and Proto-history in India, New Delhi, 1974.

7. **Presided over :**

(*i*) The First Madhya Pradesh Itihas Parishad, Bhopal.

(*ii*) The Section of Archaeology and History, Gujarat Sahitya Parishad, Calcutta, 1961.

(*iii*) The Section of Archaeology, Gujarat Research Society, Ahmedabad, 1963.

(*iv*) First Maharashtra Itihas Parishad, Bombay 1963.

(*v*) The First Archaeological Society of India, Varanasi, 1968.

(*vi*) The Second Archaeological Society of India, Patna 1969.

(*vii*) The Section of Prehistoric Industries in the Symposium on "Homo Sapiens and Environmental Changes" organized by the UNESCO, Paris, Sept., '69.

(*viii*) The Section of Anthropology and Archaeology, 57th Indian Science Congress, Kharagpur, 1970.

(*ix*) Gujarat Itihas Parishad, Dwarka, 1971.

(*x*) The Conference on the Lower Palaeolithic Cultures of Asia, and South-East Asia, Montreal and Chicago, IXth Anthropological and Ethnographical Congress, 1973.

8. **Membership of Learned Societies :**

(*i*) Elected member of the Permanent Council of the International Congress of Prehistoric and Protohistoric Societies, 1961—

(*ii*) Nominated Honorary Member of Institute, Italiano Di Prehistoria E Protohistoria, Italy, 1962—

(*iii*) Elected Honorary Fellow, Archaeological Society of India, 1968—

(*iv*) Life Member of the Asiatic Society, Bombay—

(*v*) Life Member, Bhandarkar Oriental Research Institute, Poona.

(*vi*) Life Member, Linguistic Society of India.

(*vii*) Life Member and Chairman of the Archaeological Society of India.

(*viii*) Member of the Advisory Board of Archaeology :

(*a*) Government of India 1955-1975.

(*b*) Government of Maharashtra 1955-1974.

(*c*) Government of Gujarat since 1964.

(*d*) Government of Madhya Pradesh 1966-74.

(*e*) Government of Uttar Pradesh since 1969.

Nominated as a Member of :

(*i*) The Archaeological Delegation to the U.S.S.R. in 1963-64.

(*ii*) Cultural Delegation to Yugoslavia in 1966.

(*iii*) Government of India Delegation to the International Congress of Orientalists, Ann Arbor, Michigan, U.S.A. August 1967, and Paris, 1973.

(*iv*) Advisory Editor of *World Archaeology*, published by the Southampton University, U.K.

9: **Excavation & Explorations :**

Invited by the Director General of Archaeology in India to conduct excavations and explorations in 1941. Since then the following sites have been excavated, and numerous explored all over India, excluding those in Kashmir, and near Kanyakumari, Tamil Nadu.

EXCAVATIONS AT

Gujarat

1.	Langhnaj	....	1942, 1944-49, 1962-63
2.	Akhaj	...	1947-48
3.	Valasna	...	1947-48
4.	Dwa Rangpur	....	1947-48
5.	Dwarka	....	1963
6.	Somnath (Prabhas)	...	1972, 1975-77

Maharashtra

1.	Kolhapur	...	1945-46
2.	Jorwe	...	1946-51
3.	Nasik	...	1950-51

4. Nevasa	....	1954-56, 1958-61	155
5. Chirki	...	1969-70	
6. Inamgaon	...	1969-71; 1972-74	

Madhya Pradesh

1. Maheshwar ... 1953-54
2. Navdatoli ... 1953-54; 1957-59
3. Tripuri ... 1966
4. Koyatha ... 1968-69

Mysore-Karnataka

1. Sangankal 1947; 1965
2. Tekkalkota ... 1964

Andhra

1. Betamcharla ... 1969

Rajasthan

Ahar ... 1961-62

10. Lectures Delivered

(A) Extension Lectures

(*i*) Kannada Research Institute, Karnatak Dharwar, 1955.
(*ii*) Punjab University, Chandigarh, 1960.
(*iii*) Banaras Hindu University, Varanasi, 1965.
(*iv*) Saugar University, 1967.
(*v*) Marathwada University, 1967.
(*vi*) Nagpur University, 1968.
(*vii*) Andhra University, Waltair 1972.

(B) *National Lecturer, University Grants Commission*

(*i*) Delhi University, Delhi 1974.
(*ii*) Jawaharlal Nehru University, Delhi, 1974.
(*iii*) Gujarat Vidyapeeth, Ahmedabad, 1973.
(*iv*) The University of Calicut, Calicut, 1974.
(*v*) Karnatak University, Dharwar, 1974.

(C) *Memorial Lectures*

(*i*) Thakkar Vassonji Memorial Lectures, University of Bombay, 1944. (Six lectures on the *Historical Geo-*

156

graphy and Cultural Ethnogrophy of Gujarat).
 (*ii*) Bhagwanlal Indraji Memorial Lectures, University of Bombay, 1960. (Six Lectures on *"The Prehistory and Proto-History of India & Pakistan"*.
(*iii*) First Heras Memorial Lectures, 'St. Xaviers' College, Bombay, 1960 (*Indian Archaeology Today*).
(*iv*) Thakkar Vassanji Memorial Lectures, University of Bombay, 1965 (Latest contributions and the Prehistoric and Historic Archaeology of Gujarat).
 (*v*) Rao Bahadur Gaurishankar Ozha Lectures, Sahitya Samsthan, Rajasthan Vidyapeeth, Udaipur, 1969. (Three Lectures "On Early Man and his Successors in Rajasthan).
(*vi*) Dr D. N. Majumdar Memorial Lectures on New Archaeology, "Its Scope and Application to India" under the auspices of the Ethnographic Society, Lucknow, 1974.
(*vii*) Heras Memorial Lectures, St. Xaviers College, Bombay, 1974. "On Prehistoric Art in India."
(*viii*) Bhaitaibhai Memorial Lectures on "Prehistoric Colonization in India" at Vallabh Vidyanagar, 1974.

(D) *Hon. Tagore Professor.* The M.S. University of Baroda, 1960-65

11. Publications :

 (*i*) Independently   (*ii*) Jointly
(*ii*) Independent Publications (Books only).
    (A) *Original Research—Exploration & Excavation*
        (*a*) *Investigations in the Prehistoric Archaeology of Gujarat*, Baroda, 1946.
        (*b*) *Excavations at Langhnaj,* 1944-47, Poona 1964.
        (*c*) *Mesolithic and Pre-Mesolithic Industries at Sangankal*; Poona 1966.

    (B) Original Research—Collections of Data and Interpretation.
        (*a*) *The University of Nalanda,* Madras, 1934; 2nd Revised Edition, New Delhi 1973.
        (*b*) *Archaeology of Gujarat,* Bombay, 1939.

(c) *Historical Geography and Cultural Ethnography of Gujarat* (Study of Place and Personal Names from Inscriptions) Poona, 1949.

(d) *Indian Archaeology Today*, 1964.

(e) *Prehistory and Proto-history of India & Pakistan Bombay*, 1963.

(f) *Ramayana : Myth or Reality :* New Delhi 1973.

(g) *Prehistory and Proto-History of India & Pakistan*, Revised Edition, New Poona, 1974.

(h) *New Archaeology : Its Scope and Application in India*, Lucknow, 1977.

(i) *Prehistory in India*, New Delhi, 1977.

(j) Prehistoric Art in India (In Press).

(C) *Critical Interpretation (Gujarati).*

(a) *Archaeology and the Ramayana*, Ahmedabad, 1973.

(b) *The Dawn of Civilization in Undivided India*, Ahmedabad, 1977.

(D) *Booklets and Primers*

(a) *Introduction to Archaeology*, Poona, 1965.

(b) *Stone Age Tools, Their techniques and Probable functions*, Poona, 1965.

(c) *Indus Civilization* (Gujarati), Bombay, 1967.

(d) *Mahabharat and Ramayana—Fancy or History ?*   Bombay 1977.

(E) *Joint Publications* (*Report on Excavations*)

(a) *Excavation at Kolhapur*, Poona.

(b) *Excavations at Nasik and Jorwe*, Poona.

(c) *Excavations at Maheshwar and Navdatoli*, Poona, 1955.

(d) *From History to Prehistory at Nevasa*, Poona, 1960.

(e) *Excavations at Ahar (Tambavati)* Poona, 1969.

(f) *Chalcolithic Nevdatoli*, Poona, 1971.

(g) *Excavations at Inamgaon* (In Press).

158 Research Papers :

N. B. P. before the name of the article stands for 'Popular'.

Archaeology General :

P. 1. 1938 'Archaeology for the masses', *Illustrated Weekly of India.*

P. 2. 1938 'Gold for a Merchant Prince' *Illustrated Weekly of India.*

P. 3. 1939 'Archaeological Exploration in Gujarat' *The New Review.* pp. 363-368.

4. 1940 'The Story of stone of the Great Rennunciation of Neminatha', *Indian Historical Quarterly.* Vol. XVI. pp. 314-19.

P. 5. 1940 'Buddhism is Kathiawar', *Buddha Prabha.*

6. 1942 'Cultural Significance of the Personal names in the Early Inscriptions of the Deccan', *Bulletin of the Deccan College Research Institute,* Vol. III, pp. 340-91.

7. 1943 'Notes on Cultural Geography and Ethnography of Gujarat', *Journal of the Gujarat Research Society,* Vol. V, No. 4 Oct. 1943 pp. 1-3-

8. 1945 'A Brief Summary of Studies in Historical Geography and Cultural Ethnography of Gujarat', *Journal of the Gujarat Research Society,* Vol. VII, No. 4 (Oct. 1945) pp.147-63.

9. 1947 'On the Origin of Gurjaras', *Journal of the Gujarat Research Society,* (April & July) pp. 166.

10. 1947 'Origin of Bombay' *Journal of University of Bombay.* Vol. XV, pt. 4, Jan. 1947, pp. 1-4.

11. 1950 'Cultural Significance of Saddle Guerns'. *Journal of the Anthropological Society of Bombay,* (1950) pp. 1-5.

12. 1957 'Rasbha of Adinatha', *Jaina Antiquary,* March-April, 1957.

13. 1957 'Saddle Querna and Stratigraphy', *Journal* of Royal Asiatic Society, pp. 209-12 (with S. B. Deo).

14. 1957 'Imported Mediterranean Amphorae', *JRAS,* pp. 207-208.

P. 15 1958 'The Snake in Indian Mythology' *Bhavan's* **159**
             Journal, Vol. V, No. II (Dec. 28, 1958)
             pp 57-61.

16. 16. 1958 'Houses and Habitations through the Ages',
             Bulletin of the Deccan College Research Insti-
             tute, Vol. 20 (1-4) pp. 137-63.

17. 1960 'Lata, its Historical and Cultural Significance',
             Journal of the Gujarat Research Society, Vol.
             XXII, No. 4/88 (Oct. 1960) 325-335.

P. 18. 1962 'Archaeology of Poona and its surroundings',
             38th All-India Medical Conference Souvenir
             (Poona 1962) pp. 6-12.

P. 19. 1962 'An Archaeologist's Suggestion to Universities',
             Anthropology Exhibition Souvenir, Social,
             Science Association, Madras, July 1962, pp.
             69-72

P. 20. 1963 'The Origin and Development of Writing',
             Pushpanjali, Vol, I, No. 2, Dec. 1963, pp. 95-
             98.

21. 1963 'Mahismati and Maheshwar,, *Journal of Indian*
             History, Vol. XLI, pp. 337-48.

22. 1963 'Archaeology and Tradition', *Indica,* Vol. I,
             No. I. pp. 3-18.

P. 23. 1963 'Report on Dwarka Excavations', *Times of*
             India, 19. 5. 1963.

P. 24. 1963 'Dwarka in Tradition and Archaeology'. *Times*
             of India, 2. 6. 1963.

25. 1964 'Antiquity of Modern Dwarka or Dwarka in
             Literature and Archaeology', *Journal of the*
             Asiatic Society of Bombay, (Dr. Bhau Daji
             Special Vol.) 1964, pp. 74-84.

26. 1964 'Traditional Indian Chronology and C-14
             dates of Excavated sites', *Journal of India*
             History, Vol. XIII, Part III, Dec. 1964, 635-
             650.

P. 27. 1964 'Radio Carbon Dating in Archaeology',
             Science Reporter, Vol. I, No. 10 (1964) pp.
             358-61 and 367.

P. 28. 1964 'Evolution of two Ancient Civilization', *Times*
             of India, 11. 10. 1964.

P. 29. 1965 'Art in Pottery', *Pushpanjali,* Vol. II, Dec.

160

1965, pp. 56-58.

P. 30. 'India's Language', *Times of India*, 3. 5. 1965.

31. 1966 'Review of Environment and Archaeology', *Current Anthrology*, Vol. 7, No. 4. 1966, pp. 501-14.

P. 32. 1966 'Puranas and Archaeology', *Bhavan's Journal Annual* Vol. XIII, No. 2, Aug. 4, 1966.

P. 33. 1966 'Recent Excavations and Past Legends of India', *Conspecious* No. 2, 1966 (*Quarterly Journal of the India International Centre, New Delhi.*)

34. 1966 'Archaeologi in India during the year 1965', *INDICA*, Vol. 3, Sept. 1966, No. 2, pp. 85-94.

P. 35. 1066 'Socio—economic and Geographical Background of Khajuraha', *Journal of Indian History*, Vol. XLIV, No. 130, April 1966.

36. 1969 'Problems in Indian Archaeology and Methods and Techniques and Plans to tackle them', *World Archaeology*, 1 (1969) pp. 29-39.

37. 1970 'The human and Functional Approach in Archaeology', Presidential address, *57th Indian Archaeological Congress*, Section of Anthropology and Archaeology (Kharagpur), 1970.

38. 1972 'Early man and his Environment', *INDICA*, Vol. 9, pp. 1-13.

39. 1972 'The Progress of Man', *INDICA* Vol. 9, Sept. 1972 pp. 69-82.

40. 1973 'The Beginning of Civilization in Rajasthan', *INDICA*, Vol. 10, 1973, pp. 1-24.

41. 1973 'The Beginning of Civilization in Madhya Pradesh', *Journal of Indian History*, 1973. pp. 25-56.

P. 42. 1973 'Excavations in Maharashtra', *Lokrajya*, Feb. 73.

43. 1973 'Indian Archaeology Since Independence', *BDCRI*, Vol. XXXIV, 161-68.

44. 1976 'Heras, The Archaeologist', *INDICA*. Vol. 13, pp. 3-12.

Sanskrit

45. 1966 'Kundmala and Uttararamcar ita', *Journal of*

pp. 322-34.

46. 1973 'The Ur (Original) Ramayana or Archaeology and the Ramayana' in Indogentaguns-1971. Ed. by Herbert Hartel and Voeker Mueller pp. 151-60, wisebaden. ·

47. 1974 'A Hyper Critical Study of the Ramayana', *Prachya Pratibha* Vol. II, No. 2, pp. 1-13.

48. 1976 'Archaeology and the Ramayana', (Full and revised study of the subject), *Prachya Pratibha*, Vol. IV, No, 1, pp. 1-21.

Epigraphy

49. 1936 'Short Notes : The word 'Satram' in the Gadha (Jasdan) Inscription of Mahaksatrapa Rudrasena, year 126, or 127 and a note on the Kstrapa inscriptions from Andhau, Cutch', *Journal of the Bombay Branch of the Royal Asiatic Society*, No. S. Vol. 12, (1939), pp. 104-106.

50. 1937 'The Superious Gurjara Grants of the Saka years 400, 415 and 417', *Journal of the Bombay Branch*, *Royal Asiatic Society*, N.S. Vol. XIII, pp. 21-22.

51. 1937 'Inscriptions of Gujarat—An Epigraphic Survey', *Journal of the University of Bombay*, Vol. VI, Pt. I (July 1937) pp. 75-86.

52. 1939 'XXII the Century Gold Gilt Copper-Board
     1940 Inscriptions and Sculptures from Nepal', *Bulletin of the Deccan College Research Institute*, Vol. I, No. 1. pp. 45-59.

53. 1941 'A New Copper-plate Grant of Kadamba Ravivarma : 12th Year', *New Indian Antiquary*, Vol. IV, No. 5. (Aug. 1941) pp. 178-81.

54. 1941 'Six Silahara Inscriptions in the Prince of
     1941 Wales Museum', *Epigraphia Indica*, Vol. XXV, pp. 269-281 (with B.S. Upadhyaya).

55. do— 'An Inscription of Jaitugi, Saka 1188', *Epigraphia Indica*, No. XXVI, pp. 127-130.

56. 1941 'A Copper-plate Grant of Chalukya Vijaya-
     1942 ditya : Saka 632', *Epigraphia Indica* Vol. XVII, 322-26.

162

57. do— 'A Stone Inscription of Yadava Ramachandra: Saka 1222', *Epigraphia Indica*, Vol. XXVI, No. 4. pp. 282.

58. do— 'Dohad Stone Inscription of Mahamuda (Begarha), V.S. 1545, Saka 1410', *Epigraphia Indica*, Vol. XXVI, pp. 212-225.

59.59. -do- Hilol plates of year 470', *Epigraphia Indica*, Vol. XXIV, No. 33, pp. 213-218.

60. 1969 'An Early Beahmi Cave Inscription from Pala'. *Epigraphia Indica*, Vol. XXXVIII, pp. 167-68. (with Mrs. S. Gokhale)

61. 1975 'Early Epigraphical Evidence of the Prevalence of Jainism in Gujarat', Western Maharashtra and Andhra Pradesh', *Prachya Pratibha*, Vol. II, No. 1, pp. 109.

Numismatics :

62. 1939 'A Rare Gold Coin of Huviska', *JNSI*, Vol. 1, pp. 9-10.

63. 1940 'Three New Specimens, of the Rare Variety of Eran. Ujjayani Coin,' *JNSI*, Vol. II, 1940, pp. 81-82.

64. 1952 'A New Type of Satavahan Coin From Nasik', *JNSI*, Vol. XIV, pp, 1-2.

65. 1953 'Coins from Nasik Excavations'. *JNSI*, Vol. XV, 1953, pp. 1-8.

66. 1954 'Ten Tiny Silver Punch-marked (Raupys Mashaka) Coins from Maheshwar', *JNSI*, Vol. XVI, 1954, pp. 1-3.

67. 1955 'Copper Punch-marked Coins from Nagari', *JNSI*, Vol. XVII, 1955, pp. 1-28.

Prehistory :

68. 1942 'In Search of Early Man Along the Sabarmati', *Journal of the Gujarat Research Society*, 1942.

69. 1943 'Pre and Proto-history of Gujarat', *The Glory That was Gujaradesa*, Pt. 1, pp. 12-40.

70. 1944 'The Second Gujarat Prehistoric Expedition : A Preliminary Account of the Search of Microlithic man in Gujarat', *New Indian Antiquary*, Vol. VINo. 1, (April 1944) pp.

1-5. (With Mrs. Iravati Karve).   163

71. 1945 'Studies in Prehistory of the Deccan (Maharashtra) : A Survey of the Godavari and the Kadva near Nipad', *Bulletin of the Deccan College Research Institute*, Vol. IV, No. 3, pp. 1-6.

72. 1945 'The First Gujarat Prehistoric Expedition,' *Bibliography of Indological Studies prepare by Prof. G. M. Moraes*.

73. 1945 'Studies in Prehistory of the Deccan (Maharashtra) a further Survey of the Godavari (March 1944)', Bulletin of the Deccan College Research Institute Vol. VI and No. 3, March 1965, pp. 131-137.

74. 1946 'A Palaeolithic Handadze from the Sabarmati Valley', *Journal of the University of Bombay*, Vol. IV, Pt. IV. (Jan. 1946). pp 8-10.

P. 75. 1947 'They Used Brain Surgery 10,000 years ago,' *Continental Daily Mail*, Paris 14.6. 1947.

P. 76. 1947 'Life in the Stone Age in India,' *The Hindu*, Sept. 14, 1947.

77. 1949 'Eearly Primitive Microlithic Culture and people of Gujarat' *American Anthropologist*, pp.. 28-34, (with Iravati Karve).

78. 1950 'Studies in the Prehistory of Karnataka,' *Bulletin of the Deccan College Research Institute*, Vol. XI, (1950-51) pp. 56-82 with Subha Rao and R. V. Joshi).

79. 1953 'Ancient and prehistoric Maharashtra,' *Journal of the Bombay Branch of Royal Asiatic Society*, Vol. XXVII, pt. 1, pp. 99-106

80. 1955 'Excavations at Langhnaj,' Gujarat *Man* Vol. IV, (Feb. 1955) pp. 33.

81. 1956 'The Microlithic Industry of Langhnaj, Gujarat,' *Journal of the Gujarat Research Society*, Vol. XVIII, No. 4 (Oct. 1956), pp. 275-84.

82. 1956 'Nathdwara: A Palaeolithic Site in Rajputana,' *Journal of the Palaeontological Society of India* Inaugural No. Vol. 1, (1956), pp. 99-100.

83. 1957 'Stone Age Cultures of Malwa,' *Journal of the Palaeontological Society of India*, Lucknow

164

(1957), D. N. Wadia Jubilee Number, Vol 2 pp. 183-89, (With A. P. Khatri).

84. 1957 'Is Soan Flake Industry?, *Journal of Asiatic Society of Bengal*, (Science), Vol. XXII, 16-62.

85. 1958 'The Middle Palaeolithic Culture of the Deccan-Karnataka and Central India,' *Journal of the Palaeontological Society*, (with K. D. Banerjee).

P. 87. 1962 'Prehistory and Archaeology in India', *Navroz Annual*, 1962 pp. 127-74.

P. 88. 1963 'Stone Age finds in Saurashtra : Link with Harappan Era', *Times of India*, 28. 4. 1963.

89. 1963 'Prehistory in India', *The Indo-Asian Culture*, Vol. XI, No. 3, (Jan. 1963), pp. 269-278.

P. 90. 1963 'The Story of Man in Poona 1,50,000 years ago', *Times of India*, 26. 4. 1963.

91. 1964 'Middle Stone Age Culture in India and Pakistan', *Science*, Vol. 146, No. 3642, pp. 365-75, 16th Oct.

P. 92. 1965 'Prehistoric Migration in South India', *Times of India*, 28. 3. 1965.

93. 1965 'Early Stone Age in Saurashtra', in *Diputacion Provincial De Barcelona Institute De Prehistory Archaeologia*, *Barcelona*, 1965, Monographiss XVI, pp. 327-46.

P. 94. 1965 'Links with Stone Age near Bellary', *The Hindu*, 3. 5. 1965.

95. 1965 'Aryans in the Gangetic Valley', (Dr Sampurnanand Felicitation Vol.) pp. 41-44.

96. 1966 'Prehistory and Proto-history of India', *Att, VI Congress Internaziounate Della Scienza Prehistoriche a Protohistoriche Seize* V-VIII.

97. 1966 'Prehistoric Ahmednagar', *Studies in Indian Culture*, *Dr Ghulam Yazdani Commemoration Volume*, Ed. By Prof. H.K. Sherwani, Hyderabad, A. P. 1966, pp. 39-42.

98. 1966 'Early Stone Age in Poona', *Studies in Prehistory*, *Robert Bruce Foote Memorial Volume*, Ed. Sen and Ghose, 1966. pp. 77-89.

99. 1966 'Sir Rustom and Research in Anthropology', *The Journal of Anthropological Society of*

Bombay, (New Series), Vol. XII, No. 1,1966, 165
00.56 ff.

100. 1966 'A Revised Study of the Soan Culture', *The Anthropologist*, Vol. XIV, No. 1. pp. 1-40.

101. 1968 'Beginning of Civilization in South India', *II Int. Conf. on Tamil Studies*, pp. 1-15 (Separate Brochure).

102. 1969 'Early Man in the India'. *JAS, Bombay*, 1966-67 (New Series) pp. 173-181.

103. 1969 'Prehistoric Man and Primitives in South Gujarat and Konkan', *Journal of the Antropological Society of Bombay*, New Series, Vol. XII, No. 1, 1966, pp. 34-38.

104. 1970 'The Middle Palaeolothic Cultures of India, Central and Western Asia and Europe', *Central Asia* 1970 Ed. by Amalendu Guha, pp. 25-52 (With Illustrations and maps).

105. 1971 'Earliest Traces of Man in Bengal', *The Times of India*, January 24, 1971.

106. 1971 'The Prehistoric Background of Uttar Pradesh', *Eastern Anthropologists* Vol. XXIV, No. 1. Jan. April, 1971, pp. 25-38.

107. 1971 'The Philosophy of Archaeology in India or Theoritical and Methodical Approaches in Archaeological Inter-pretations in India', *Journal of Indian History*, Vol. XLVIII, April, 1970, pp. 27-42.

108. 1971 'Punjab and the Aryans or Prehistoric Punjab', *Prof. K. A. N. Shastri Felicitation Volume*, Madras, 1971 pp. 259-269.

109. 1971 'Early Man in Ice Age Kashmir', *Science Today* December 1971.

110. 1971 'New Evidence for Early Man in Kashmir', *Current Anthropology*, Vol. 2, No. 4. pp. 558-62.

111.   'The Handaxe Industry in the Punjab', in *Perspectives in Palaecanthropology*, Ed. by Ashok K. Ghosh, Calcutta, 213-19.

112. 1972 'Puranas and Prehistory of Bihar', *JIH*, XLVIII, Dec. 1970, pp. 461-68.

113. 1974 'The Handaxe Industry in the Punjab', in *Perspectives in Palaeo-anthropology*, Ed. A. K.

Ghosh, pp. 213-19.

114. 1976 'Early and Middle Palaeolithic Culture in India and Pakistan', is Colloque VII to Palaeolithique INFERIEUR at MOYEN en INDE en ASIE CENTRALE, en CHNE at Dans Sut-Est Asiatique, Nia. pp. 1-30.

115. 1977 'Prehistoric Europe', *Illustrated Weekly of India* 26th June 1977, pp. 30-33.

Proto-history :

116. 1953 'Archaeological Sequence of Central India'. *South Western Journal of Anthropology*, Vol. 9. No. 4 (1953) pp. 343-356 (with S. B. Deo and B. Subba Rao).

117. 1953 'Excavations in the Narmada Valley', *Journal of the M.S. University of Baroda*, Vol. II, No. 2.

118. 1955 'Navadatoli Dancers', *Antiquity* Vol., XXIX, pp. 28-31 (March 1955)

119. 1955 'Spouted Vessels from Navadatoli (Madhya Bharat) and Iran', *Antiquity* Vol. XXIX, pp. 12-15, June.

120. 1955 'Flat Bronze Axes from Jorwe, Ahmednagar District, Deccan', *Man*, Vol. IV, p. 1, Jan. 1955.

121. 1956 'Animal Fosists and Palaeolithic Industries from the Pravara Basin at Nevasa, District Ahmednagar', *Ancient India*, XII, pp. 35-52.

122. 1957 'The making-up of India', *Journal of the Maharaja Sayajirao University of Baroda*, Vol. VI, No., 1 (March 1957) pp. 27-32.

123. 1957 'The Excavations at Maheshwar and Nevasa and their possible bearing on the Puranic History,' *The Sardha Satabdi Commemoration*, Vol. *JAS* (1804-1954) pp. 229-239.

124. 1958 'Pre and Proto-History of Malwa', *An Introduction* Lecture delivered on the inauguration of the *Madhya Pradesh* Itihas Parishad on 10.7.58, Deccan College, Poona.

125. 1958 'New Light on the Aryan Invasion', of India: Links with Iran of 1000 B.C. Discoverd in Central India' *Illustrated London News*, Sept.,

10, 1958, pp. 478-79.   **167**

126. 1959 'A Unique Realistic Painting of the chalco-
            lithic Period in the Deccan', *Dr S.K. Belwalkar
            Felicitation* Vol. pp. 223-24.

127. 1959 'Excavations at Navdatoli and Maheshwar',
            Akashwani, 15.11.59,

128. 1959 'Four-Thousand Year Old Links Between
            Iran and Central India ; New Excavations at
            Navdatoli', *Illustrated London News*, Sept. 5,
            1959.

129. 1962 'New Links between Western Asia and the
            India of 4000 years ago : Excavations in
            'Huge' 'Dust Heap' of Ahar, Near Udaipur',
            Illustrated London News, Sept. 1, 1962, pp.
            222-25,

130. 1963 'Beginning if Civilization in Rajasthan', in
            *Second Seminar on the History of Rajasthan
            Supplement* to the M.S. College Magazine,
            p. 1-16.

131. 1963 'The Earliest Farmers in the Narmada Valley,
            The Indo-Asian Culture, Vol. XI, No. 1, pp.
            31-38.

P. 132. 1963 'Protohistory in India', *Indo-Asian Culture,*
               Vol. XI, pp. 355-60.

133. 1964 'New Light on the Indo-Aranian or Western
            Asiatic Relations between 1700 B.C.—1200
            B.C., *Artibus Asiae* Vol. XXIV, pp. 312-332.

134. 1964 'Traditional India Chronology and C-14 dates
            of Excavated sites', *Journal of Indian History,*
            Vol. XIII, pp. 635-650.

135. 1969 'Kot-Diji and Hissar III', *Antiquity*, pp.
            142-44.

P. 136. 1970 'Iranian Influence on Early Indo-Pakistani
               Cultures', *Central Asia, Indian Council of
               Cultural Relations*, New Delhi, pp. 53-74.

137. 1972 'The Chalcolithic Cultures of India', *Archae-
            ological Congress and Seminar*, Ed. by Dr S.B.
            Deo Nagpur University, Nagpur, 1972.

138. 1973 Inamgaon, 'A Chalcolithic Settlement in
            Western India' with Ansari, Z.D. and Dha-
            valikar, M.K. *Asian Perspectives*, Vol. XIV,
            pp. 139-46.

168

139. 1974 'Radio Carbon and Indian Archaeology', *BDCRI*, Vol. XXXIV pp. 161-68.

140. 1975 'The Earliest Private Shrine in Western India and its relationship with the Mother Goddess in Europe and Western Asia', Valcomina Symposium De La Prehistorique (Edizioni DEL CENTRO 1975), pp. 457-61.

141. 1975 'An Early Farmer Village in Central India', (with Z.D. Ansari and M.K. Dhavalikar), *Expedition*, Vol. 17, pp. 1-11.

142. 1976 'Ecological Background of South Asian Prehistory', Ed . K. A. R. Kennedy and G.R. Possehe, South Asia occasional papers, South Asian Programme Council University, pp. 132-65.

Survey Articles :

143. 1941 'Regional and Dynastic study of South Indian Monuments', *Bhandarkar Oriental Research Institute*, Vol. XXI, pp. 213-228.

144. 1942 'Pre-Vedic Times to Vijayanagar : A Survey of 25 years', Work in Ancient Indian History and Archaeology', *Progress of India Studies*, 1917-42. pp. 195-238. Govt. Oriental Series Class B.No., Bhandarkar Oriental Research Institute.

145. 1943 'Pre- and-Proto-History of Gujarat', In the *Glory that was Gujaradesha*, pp. 12-40.

146. 1952 'Archaeology and Indian Universities', Presidential Address Archaeology Sec. *All India Oriental Conference*, Lucknow.

147. 1952 'Archaeological Planning for Gujarat', *Presidential Address*, *Gujarat Workers' Conference*, Ahmedabad, pp. 1-9.

148. 1957 'Man in the arid and semi-arid regions of the
    1958 Peninsular India', H.D. Shankalia and R.V. Joshi, *Bulletin*, *Deccan College Research Institute* (Taraporewalla Vol. XVIII). pp. 123-36.

149. 1960 'Archaeology of Gujarat', An Introduction, pp. 14-20.

150. 1962 'India' in courses towards Urban Life, pp. 80-83 'From Food collection to Urbanisation

in India', *Indian Anthropology*, Asia Publishing House, pp. 66-104.

151. 1965 'The History of Man in Maharashtra : Work done and plan of work ahead', Presidential address, *First Maharashtra Itihas Parishad*, Bombay.

152. 1966 'Archaeology in India during the year 1965', *Indica*, Vol. 3, pp. 85-97.

153. 1967 'Prehistoric Culture and Remains in the Volume on History : Ancient Period, *Gazetteer of India, Maharashtra State*, Part 1, pp. 1-56.

154. 1968 'Historical Geography from Inscriptions', *Review of Indological Research in last 75 years* (M.M. Siddheshwar Shastri Chitrava Felicitation Volume), pp. 249-288.

155. 1970 'History of Jamnagar District' in *Gazetteer of India, Gujarat State, Jamnagar District*, pp. 51-56.

156. 1971 'History of Kutch' in *Gazetteer of India, Gujarat State, Kutch District*, pp. 65-109

157. 1971 'Indian Influence on the World', *The Times* of India, 15th August 1971, (Review, Vivekanand Cenetenary Vol).

158. 1971 'Underwater Archaeology', (Review, *The Times of India*, 7.2'.1971).

159. 1971 'The Man in Maharashtra', *Bhavan's Journals*, 9.4.1970 and 20.9.1970, pp. 53-58.

160. 1972 'Archaeology for the Masses', *The Times of India*, June, 1972.

161. 1972 'Vidharabha Diggings', *The Times of India*, 3.9.72.

162. 1972 'Maitraka—Kalina Gujarat', (by Dr H.P. Shastri) *Vidya* pp. 1-6.

P. 163. 1972 'Not of this World' (Review, *The Times of India*) 31.1.72.

Sculpture, Iconography and Architectures :

164. 1938 'An American Fertility Figure and Lakulisa', *Indian Culture*, Vol. IV, pp. 358-59.

165. 1938 'A Unique Image of Surya', *Jornal of University of Bombay*, Vol. VI, pp. 50-57.

166. 1939 'Rare Figure of Visnu from Gujarat', *Journal*

of University of Bombay, Vol. VII, pp. 1-16.

167.   1939   'Two Rare Images of Buddishist Trantric Deity Padmanartersvara', *Indian Historical Quarterly*, Vol. XV, pp. 278-80.

168.   1939   'An Unusual form of a Jain Goddess', *Jain Antiquary*, Vol. IV, pp. 86-88.

169.   1939   'Six Different types of Canesa Figures', *Journal of Indian History*, Vol. XVIII, pp. 188-94.

170.   1939   'Jaina Iconography', *New Indian Antiquary*, Vol. II, pp. 497-520.

171.   1940   'The Ambarnath Temple' *BDCRI*, Col. I, pp. 170-77.

172.   1941   'The early Medieval Temples of Gujarat and Treatise on Architecture', *Journal of Gujarat Research Society*, Vol. III, pp. 1-4.

173.   1942   'Jain Monuments, from Deogarh,' *Journal of the Indian Society Oriental Art*, Vol. II, 97-104.

174.   1944   'Iconographical Elements in the Maha-bharata', *BDCRI*, Vol. V, pp. 149-61 (V.S. Sukhatankar Vol.)

175.   1946   'The Antiquity of Glass Bangles in India', *BDCRI*, (*K.N. Dikshit Memorial Vol.*) Vol. VIII, Nos. 3-4, pp. 252-259.

176.   1948   'A Unique VI Century Inscribed Sati Stele from Sangli, Kolhapur State', *BDCRI*, Vol. III, pp. 161-166 (with M.G. Dikshit). XXI, pp. 10-11.

177.   1953   'Vitthala and Hari, *Journal of University of Bombay*. Vol. I.

178.   1960   'The Nude Goddess of Shameless Women', in Western Asia, India and South-Eastern Asia, *Artibus Asia* Vol. XXIII, 23.

179.   1966   'A Unique Iron Spear-head from Tripuri', *Bulletin of the Museum and Picture Gallery, Baroda*, Vol. XX.

P. 180.   1969   'Terracotta Art of India', *Marg*, Vol. XXIII (with Dr M. K. Dhavalikar)

P. 181.   1970   'Iron Age in Maharashtra', *The Times of India*, August 16, 1970.

182.   1970   'Digambar Jain Tirthankaras from Maheshwar and Newasa', *Acharya Vijayavallathasuri*

Comm. Vol, pp. 116-120.

P. 183. 1970 'Cultural Outposts of India', II, *March of India*, (Adopted from the Broadcast of AIR), pp. 24-28.

184. 1970 'Stone Age Hill Dwellers of South India', I *INDICA*, Vol. 1-2, pp. 129-140.

185. 1967 'Research Report—The Socio-economic Significance of the Lithic Blade Industry of Navdatoli, Madhya Pradesh', *Current Anthoropology*, Vol. 8, pp, 262-268.

P. 186. 1967 'Archaeology and the Ramayana', *The Times of India*, 26. 12. 1967.

187. 1967 'Prehistory and Proto-history in India between 1962-66', *Journal of Indian History*, Vol. XLV, pp. 99-107.

P. 188. 1967 'Isolation and Survival : Easter Island', Review of the Nowregian Archaeological Expedition to the Eastern Island and the pacific Vol. 2, 1965. *The Times of India*, Sunday Ed. 24. 12 1967.

189. 1967 'Nava-Saurashtra-Mandala', *Jouranal of the Gujarat Research Socity*, Vol. XXIX, pp. 229-46.

190. 1968 'History of Kutch', *Journal of Gujarat Research Society*, Vol. XXX.

191. 1976 'Morphological Evolution of Nataraja', *The Eastern Anthropologist*, Vol. 29, pp. 119-42.

192. 1976 'Nataraja in the Mahabharata', *Subrahmanyam Felicitation Volume*, pp. 51-56.

P. 193. 1977 'Evolution of the State Architectur', (Review) *Times of India*.

P. 194. 1977 'Modern Museum', (Review), *Times of India*.

Archaeology and National Problems :

P. 1. 1966 'To Kill or not to kill (the cow)', *The Times of India*, Sunday 18. 12. 66.

P. 2. 1967 'The Cow Slaughter in History', *Seminar*, 93, May 1967. pp. 6-16, (this is documented).

P. 3. 1967 'Cultural Divisions of India', *Science Today* August.

P. 4. 1967 'India's Language', *Education and Culture*, Vol. IV.

172 P. 5. 1967 'Our National Monuments', *The Times of India*, 30. 11. 1967.

P. 6. 1977 'Election Results in Historical perspective', *Bhavan's Journal*, June 19, 1977. pp. 55-56.

Articles in Gujarati (1933-1976)

१.   १९३३   "मोहન-જોદડો અને સિન્ધુ નદીના તટની ખ્રિસ્તપૂર્વ ५००० વર્ષ પહેલાંનો સંસ્કૃતિ" **પ્રસ્થાન**, ભાગ १५-१६ પા૦ १२२-१२૬, २४५-५४

२.   १९३३   "કલા અને સંસ્કૃતિના પ્રચારમાં નાલન્દાનો પાલો" **વસન્ત** પા૦ १३०-३५

३.   १९३५   "કુન્દમાલા અને ઉત્તરરામચરિતા વચ્ચેનું સામ્ય" **પ્રસ્થાન** ભાગ १०, પા૦ ३२२-२૬

४.   १९३૬   "કાઠિયાવાડમાં પ્રાચીન જૈન શિષ્યોની ઉપલબ્ધિ" **જૈન સત્યપ્રકાશ**, (વિશેષાંક) પા૦ १४૬-५२

५.   १९४१   "પુરાતત્વની દષ્ટિયે ગુજરાતના પ્રાચીન ધર્મો" **ત્રૈમાસિક**, પુ૦ ખં૦ ४ પા૦ ५૮-૬१ અને કુ૦ ૬ અં૦ १, પા૦ ૮૬-१०१

૬.   १९४४   "ગુજરાતમાં પ્રાગૈતિહાસિક માનવ" **માનસી**, પા૦ १७-२०

७.   १९४७   "કાંચની બંગડીની પૌરાણિકતા" **અધ્યોગ** (અહમદાવાદ) દીપાવલી અંક, પા૦ १७-१૮, १३५-४०

૮.   १९४७   "ગુજરાતમાં પાષાણયુગોની સંસ્કૃતિ" **ગુજરાતમિત્ર** અને **ગુજ-રાતદર્પણ** (દીવાલી અંક)

૯.   १९५४   "પ્રાચીન ગુજરાતનાં સંસ્કૃતિ સૂચવતા વ્યક્તિનામો" **ગુજરાત-મિત્ર** અને **ગુજરાતદર્પણ**, (દીપાવલી અંક) પા૦ ૬५

१०.   १९५૬   "પ્રાચીન ગુજરાતના રાજકીય વિભાગો" **ગુજરાતમિત્ર** અને **ગુજરાત દર્પણ**, (દિવાલી અંક) પા૦ १७

११.   १९५७   "મહેશ્વર-નાવડાટોલીની ३५०० વર્ષ જુની તામ્ર-પાષાણયુગી સંસ્કૃતિ અને આર્યોનું ભારતામાં આગમન" **જ૦ઑફ ગુજ૦-રી૦ સોસા૦**, પા૦ ३२३-३૬

१२.   १९५૮   "મહેશ્વરની તામ્રપાષાણયુગની સંસ્કૃતિ" **અખંડઆનંદ**, એપ્રૈલ, २७-४२

१३.   १९૬०   "પુરાણવસ્તુ સંશોધન શાસ્ત્ર" **સંસ્કૃતિ**, પા૦ २૬१-૬४

१४.   १९૬१   "કુમ્ભારની કલા" **કુમાર**, માર્ચ, પા૦ ૫२

174 १५. १९६२ ''मानव इतिहास'' (इतिहास-पुरातत्त्व विभागानां प्रमुखनुं व्याख्यान गुजराती साहित्य परिषद २१ मुं॰ अधिवेशन कलकत्ता

१६. १९६२-६३ ''पुरातत्त्व संशोधन : अभ्यास अने आलेखन'' ज॰ ऑफ दी गुज॰ री॰ सोमा॰ १९६२-६३, पा॰ ६५-७२

१७. १९६३ ''नालंदा'' समर्पण, ऑक्टोबर, पा॰ १३६-४०

१८. १९६३ ''सौराष्ट्रमां मानव संस्कृतिनों प्रारम्भ अने विकास'' समर्पण जून, पा॰ २२-२६, १०५-१०७

१९. १९६३ ''पुराणो अने पुरातत्त्वनी दृष्टिये द्वारका'' समर्पण, जुलाई, २२-२८

२०. १९६७ ''गुजरातमां प्रागैतिहासिक संशोधन'' बुद्धिप्रकाश, पा॰ ३७१-३७५

२१. १९६८ ''गुजरातनुं पुरातत्त्व'' श्री दिल्ली गुजराती समाज हीरक महोत्सव स्मृतिग्रन्थ

२२. १९६८ ''भारतना सांस्कृति विभागो'' समर्पण, फे॰ब्रु पा॰ १-१०

२३- १९६८ ''सौराष्ट्रनी भूस्तररचना अथवा शैलो'' पथिक, जुलै॰ आंग पा॰ ३१-३५

२४. १९६८ ''सौराष्ट्रनां पाषाणयुगो' पथिक, जुलै॰-आग॰ पा॰ ४१-४५

२५. १९६८ ''भरूचमां बौद्धधर्म अने बौद्धधर्मीयों'' पथिक, सप्टे॰ पा॰ १५

२६. १९६८ ''कच्छमां आदि अश्मयुग'' पथिक, ऑक्टो॰ पा॰ ४१-४५

२७. १९६८ महाराष्ट्रमां जैन धर्मनो प्रचार'', २३०० वर्ष पहेलां थयो हतो: पाल्यनो शिलालेख'' मुंबई समाचार, २५ डिसं॰

२८. १९७१ नवसुराष्ट्रमण्डल'' पथिक (दिपोत्सवी अंक) पा॰ ३३-३७

२९. १९७१ ''पुरातत्त्वो अने पुराणो'', महाभारत अने रामायण,'' स्वाध्याय, (दिपोत्सवी अंक) पा॰ ८८-११०

३०. १९७१ ''काश्मीरमां हिमयुगीन मानव'' पथिक, (दिपोत्सवी अंक) अने समर्पण (दिपोत्सवी अंक)

३१. १९७२ 'सौमनाथमां खोदकाम'' (राजकोट) फेब्रु॰, मार्च, अप्रिल

३२. ,, ''सौमनाथमां पुरातत्त्वीय खोदकाम'' प्रदर्शन बखते प्रकट थयेली पत्रिका, पा॰ २-३२

३३. ,, ''गुजरातना पाषाणयुगो'' पथिक, मे-जून, पा॰ २५-३३

३४ १९७४ ''आध्यरामायण'' कुमार, सुवर्ण ज्योति अंक, वर्ष ५०, अंक १२, डिसें॰ १९७३, पा॰ ४३६-४०

३५. ,, ''जैनधर्मनी प्राचीनता'' कुमार, मे १४६-४७ १७३

३६. ,, "लांघणज अने मोडासानो प्रागैतिहासिक अने सांस्कृतिक
        इतिहास" समर्पण जुलाई, पा० ३६-२૯, ५०-५७

३७. ., महाभारत अने पुरातत्व" साधना, दिपोत्सवी अंक,
        पा० २५-૭

३८. ,, "मोडासानी पकवेली नामांकित पकवेली भाटीनी व्यक्ति"
        प्रवासी, दिपोत्सवी अंक, पा० ૪५-૪६

३૯. १૯૭५ "डा० हसमुख साकलिया" जीवन घडवैया, नवचेतन, जुलै,
        पा० १२-१५

४०. ,, "महाभारतमां रोमनगरी" साधना, दिपोत्सवी अंक

४१. ,, महाभारतनुं युद्ध अने तेनो समय" समर्पण, दिपोत्सवी
        अंक, ४१-૪८

४२. १૯૭६ "महाभारतनुं युद्ध अने लोहयुग" गुज० इन्टरनेशनल
        (त्रिमासिक) जान्यु० फेब्रु० पा० २૭-३२

४३. ,, "लंका अने सिंहल ताम्रपत्रो अने शिलालेखोमां" पथिक,
        दिपोत्सवी अंक

४४. ,, "आपण ऐतिहासिक वारसो" पथिक, अप्रिल, पा० ५०

Articles in Marathi (1951-1977)

१. १૯५१ "प्राचीन आणि प्रागैतिहासिक महाराष्ट्र" **नवभारत** खं.
        ५, पृ. १-૬

२. १૯५३ "प्रागैतिहासिक गुजरात" **पराग**, पृ. ११-१૬

३. १૯૭६ "गुजरात, महाराष्ट्र आणि कर्नाटक यामधील सम्बन्ध आणि
        पट्टी-हट्टी" **नवभारत**, खं. ३० पा० १०-१३

४. १૯५૬ "कोल्हापुरात रोम कुंभ **सकाल**

५. ,, नेवासाचे अश्मयुगातील दोन संस्कृतिचे अवशेष"
        (आणि शां. भा. देव) **सकाल**

६. ,, नेवासे १૯५४-५૬" पूरे विद्यापीठ पत्रिका (पाणि शां.
        भा. देव)

૭. ,, "तलाजा : बौद्ध गुफा" साधना २४ मे.

८. १૯५૭ " नालंदा विद्यापीठ" **जीवन विकास**, पृ. १૬२

૯. १૯५८ महाराष्ट्रातील इतिहासपूर्व संस्कृतिया उष:काल" **जीवन
        विकास**, वर्ष ३ रे, पृ. २५८-२૬०

१०. ,, "महाराष्ट्रातील इतिहासपूर्व कालातील पहिला माणूस"
        जीवन विकास, वर्ष ३ रे, पृ. ૪८૬-५०१

११. १૯૬१ "प्राचीन ईराणी व मध्य भारतीय कलाकृनीतील साम्य"

176

रविवाल सकाल, १९ मे०

१२. १९६३ ''पाषाणयुगातील पुर्णे'' केसरी

१३. ,, ''दीड लाख वर्षांपूर्वी पुण्यात पाषाणयुगी मानव'' रविवार सकाल, १४ अप्रिल

१४. ,, ''द्वारका नगरी तीन वेळा वसविली'' सकाल, २६ मे०

१५. ,, ''दीड लाख वर्षांपूर्वी पंढरीत मानवी वस्ती'' गोकर्ण; (पंढर- पूर) ७ डिसे.

१६. १९६७ ''संस्कृत राजभाषा व प्रदेश भाषा'' सकाल ८ जाने.

१७. ,, ''पेसेफिक बेटावर मानवाच्या प्राचीन वस्तीचा पुरावा'' रविवार सकाल १० सप्टे.

१८. १९६७ ''प्राचीन भारताचे सांस्कृतिक रूप दर्शन'' सकाल, १० नोव्हें.

१९. ,, ''प्राचीन कालात करण्यांत आलेला सांस्कृतिक ऐकात्मतेषा प्रयत्न'' केसरी, २४ डिसें.

२०. १९६८ ''श्री कृष्णाची द्वारका : नवे संशोधन'' महाराष्ट्र टाईम्स ३ ऐप्रिल

२१. ,, ''रामावताराचा आणि रामायणाचा काल'' सकाल, २४ जाने.

२२. ,, ''महाराष्ट्रात अति प्राचीन कालात जैन धर्मप्रचार'' सकाल, २४ नोव्हेंम्बर

२३. १९६९ ''इनामगांव उत्खननातील नवीन मूलभूत माहिती'' (आणि अन्सारी, ढवलीकर), सकाल, २३ फेब्रु.

२४. ,, ''ताम्रपाषाणयुगीन महाराष्ट्र'' केसरी, ३३ फेब्रु.

२५. ,, ' उत्कृष्ट कोरीब शिल्पातूत तीर्थंकर नेमीनाथ यांची जीवनकथा'' स्वराज्य, १४ मे.

२६. ,, ''फलटणचे प्राचीन वैभव'' (आणि सौ. गोखले) सकाल, १५ नोव्हें.

२७. ,, ''काश्मीरमध्ये हिमयुगीन मानवाचे अवशेष'' सकाल, डिसे. २१.

२८. १९७० ' महाराष्ट्रातील उत्खनन आणि इनामगांव उत्खननाचे महत्व'' २३ फेब्रु.

२९. ,, ''महाराष्ट्रातील आध्य मानव'' केसरी, मे १०

३०. ,, ' महाराष्ट्रातील अति प्राचीन मानवी वसाहतीसम्बन्धी नवे संशोधन'' केसरी, मे १७

३१. ,, ''दुस-या अश्मयुगापासून स्थिर जीवनाला प्रारम्भ ' केसरी, मे २४.

३२. ,, ''ग्रामीण जीवनाला प्रारंभ झाल्यानंतर आढळून येणारी

३३.   ,,   "महाराष्ट्रातील आध्यानव" **केसरी,** २४ मे मानव

३४.   ,,   "महाराष्ट्रातील आध्यमानवासम्बन्धी संशोधन" **केसरी,**
              ३१ मे

३५.   ,,   "रोमचे प्राचीन आसामशी दलणवलस्श"

३६.   १६७१   "महाराष्ट्राची आदी-माता" **म. टाईम्स,** १६ मे

३७.   ,,   "अश्मयुग ते लोहयुग" (पुस्तिका) १६७१

३८.   ,,   "डेक्कन कॉलिजची दीडशे वर्ष" **स्वराज्य,** २१ ऑगस्ट

३९.   ,,   "महाराष्ट्रातील मानव" **अस्मिता महाराष्ट्राची** (संपादित)
              १६७१ पा, १-२७

४०.   १६७२   "सिन्धु संस्कृतिचे स्वरूपदर्शन" **केसरी** २, १२, १६, २६
              सप्टे.

४१.   ,,   "भिल्ल सरगम उत्खनन" **रविवार सकाळ,** फेब्रुअरी ६

४२.   ,,   "कलावस्तूंची लूटमार कशी थांबेल" **सकाळ,** २ जुलै

४३.   ,,   "भारत सरकारचा पुरातत्व विभाग जनताभिमुख होणार
              की नाही" **तरुण भारत,** ८ जुलै १६ जुलै

४४.   ,,   "दुर्भिळ भारतीय कलावस्तूंचे वर्लीमसधील संग्रहालय"
              केसरी

४५.   ,,   "पुरात-त्वीय दृष्टिकोणातून रामायणावर नवीन प्रकाश"
              १ नोव्हें. **प्रसाद** (रौप्यमहोत्सवी अंक), १ डिसें. **प्रसाद**

४६.   १६७५   "पुरात-त्वीय दृष्टिकोणातून रामायणावर नवीन प्रकाश"
              अमृत, मार्च आणि एप्रिल

४७.   ,,   "पुण्यातील आदिमानव" रौप्यमहोत्सव स्मरणिका,
              पुणे महानगरपालिका १६५०-१६७५ पृ. ४१-४५

४८.   ,,   "द्वारका आणि पुरात-त्व" **अमृत,** सप्टे. पा. १५१-५८

४९.   १६७२   "रामायणवर्ती नवीन प्रकाश" **केसरी** सप्टे.

५०.   १६७४   "पुरात-त्व संशोधन एक गुप्तचर विध्या" **कलश.**

५१.   १६७६   "महाराष्ट्राची आदि मातृका" लोकशिक्षण, एप्रिल, मे पा.३

५२.   ,,   "सालवन क्षेत्र, गोंड आणि लंका" **लोकस-ता,** ५.११.७६

५३.   ,,   "पादुका प्रसंग रामायणात नंतर" **सकाळ** ७.११.५६

५४.   १६७७   "महाभारतचा युद्ध आणि लोहयुग" **नवभारत,** जान्यु.

५५.   ,,   "रामाच्या पादुका आणि पादुका पूजेचे महत्तव" **अमृत,**
              जाने. पा. ७७-८१

१.   १६५५   "कवि कालिदास और महेश्वरी की प्राचीनता" जर्नल ओफ दी मध्यप्रदेश इतिहास परिषद भाग ४ पृ० ७-६

२.   १६५६   "नेवासाके पर्यवेक्षणका ऐतिहासिक व सांस्कृतिक महत्त्व" धर्मयुग अक्तूबर, पृ. ६-७

३.   १६६८   "जैनधर्म सम्बन्धी एक अत्यन्त महत्त्वपूर्ण शिलालेख की खोज" धर्मयुग, १६, २६ दिसम्बर, पृ. १६, १६

४.   १६६८   "मैंने प्रागैतिहासिक कालीन भारत की खोज कैसे की" धर्मयुग दिसम्बर, पृ० १६-१७

५.   ,,   "क्या आदि मानव ने मध्यप्रदेश में डेरा डाला था" धर्मयुग १२ जनवरी, पृ० १६-१७

६.   १६६६   "घने जंगलों और चट्टानों के बीच महाराष्ट्र में यह आदि मानव" धर्मयुग २६ जनवरी, पृ० १६-१७

७.   ,,   "क्या राजस्थान में कभी सागर लहरें इठलाती थी" धर्मयुग ६ फरवरी पृ० १६-१७

८.   ,,   "भारत के सबसे पुराने मानव-अस्थिपन्जर गुजरात में" धर्म-युग 23 फरवरी, पृ० 16-17

६.   ,,   "दक्षिण भारत में सभ्यता का आदि आरम्भ" धर्मयुग 23 मार्च पृ० १६-१७

१०.   ,,   यहाँ साढे तीन हजार साल पहले की मानव सभ्यता के अव-शेष मिले" धर्मयुग २२ जुलाई पृ० २०-२१

११.   ,,   "गुजराज की प्रागैतिहासिक एवं एतिहासिक संस्कृतियों का आभास चित्रों द्वारा आलेखन" धर्मयुग, १६ नवम्बर, पृ० १६-१७

१२.   ,,   "क्या तीन लाख साल पहले काश्मीर में आदमी रहता था" धर्मयुग ३० नवम्बर, पृ. १६-१७

१३.   १६७०   "कामरूप की घाटी में प्रागैतिहासिक अवशेष" धर्मयुग १६ अप्रैल पृ० १६ तथा २६ अप्रैल पृ. १६-१७

१४.   १६७१   "तूतन खामन की कब्र के तिलस्मी रहस्य" धर्मयुग, फरवरी १४, २१, २८ और मार्च ७.

१५.   १६७२   "प्रागैतिहासिक काल में पंजाब" धर्मयुग मार्च, पृ. ५ और १२

१६   ,,   "प्रागैतिहासिक काल में उत्तर प्रदेश" धर्मयुग अप्रैल, पृ. ६, १६

१७. १६७२ "प्रागैतिहासिक काल में विहार" धर्मयुग मई,

१८ ,, "पुराण रामायण और महाभारत" आजकल, अप्रैल, पृ. २-५

१६- ,, "ऐतिहासिक कला की जांच और पुरातत्व की परखनली" धर्मयुग

२०. ,, "रावण की लंका कहां थी" धर्मयुग, जून, पृ. ५-६ ३५

२१. ,, "रामायण का रचना काल" धर्मयुग मई, पृ. ६-८

२२. ,, "बंगाल में मानव का निवास कितना पुराना" धर्मयुग २ जुलाई

२३. ,, "प्रागैतिहासिक संस्कृति, पुराण और पुरातत्व का ताना-बाना" धर्मयुग, १६ जुलाई, पृ. २५-२६ ४८

२४. ,, "पश्चिम बंगाल का खेती करने वाला पुराना गाँव" धर्मयुग जुलाई,

२५. १६७५ "रामायण पुरातत्व की दृष्टि से" कादम्बिनी, जुलाई, ३६-३९

२६. १६७६ "महाभारत युद्ध कल्पित है" कादम्बिनी, जनवरी, पृ. २६-३१

२७ ,, "महाभारत का युद्ध और लौहयुग" धर्मयुग, 5 दिसम्बर, पृ. २४

२८. ,, "महाभारत का युद्ध और लौहयुग" धर्मयुग, २८ नवम्बर, पृ. २४

२६. १६७७ "रावण की लंका मध्य प्रदेश में" कादम्बिनी, अप्रैल, पृ. २४-२९

LIST OF PH.D. STUDENTS WHO WORKED UNDER DR H.D. SANKALIA

No.	Year	Name	Title of the thesis
1.	1944	D. R. Patil	Cultural History from the Vayu Purana.
2.	1947	A. V. Naik	Archaeology of the Deccan.
3.	1949	B. Subba Rao	Prehistoric and early historic Bellary.
4.	1952	S. B.Deo	History of the Jaina Monachism from Inscriptions and Literature.
5.	1952	G. A. Deleury	The Cult of Vithoba.
6.	1953	R. V. Joshi	Pleistocene Studies in the Malaprabha Basin—Prehistory and Geochronology.
7.	1954	Mrs. Sumati Mulay	Studies in the Historical and Cultural Geography and Ethnography of the Deccan.
8.	1957	K.D. Banerjee	Middle Palaeolithic Industries of the Deccan.
9.	1957	M. S. Mate	Maratha Architecture (1650-1850)
10.	1958	B.N. Chapekar	Iconographical Elements in the Mahabharata.
11.	1958	A. P. Khatri	Stone Age Cultures of Malwa.
12.	1960	Z. D. Ansari	Geometrical approach to Prehistoric and Ancient Indian Pottery.
13.	1960	Mrs. Shobhana Gokhale	Studies in the Historical and Cultural Geography and Ethnograpy of Madhya Pradesh.
14.	1960	N. Isaac	Stone Age Cultures of Kurnool.
15.	1960	C. G. Mohapatra	Stone Age Cultures of Orissa.
16.	1961	K. R. Kapre	Archaeology of the Ancient Place Names in the Deccan.

17.	1961	V. N. Mishra	Stone Age Cultures of Rajputana.
18.	1962	K. L. Lele	Studies in the Historical and Cultural Geography and Ethnography of Rajasthan.
19.	1963	Mrs. Madhur Mohini Mathur	Studies in the Historical and Cultural Geography and Ethnography of U. P.
20.	1963	M. K. Dhawalikar	Life in the Deccan as depicted in The Ajanta Paintings.
21.	1963	P. R. Sharma	Archaeology of Nepal.
22.	1963	Suresh B. Pillay	Historical and Cultural Geography and Ethnography of South India.
23.	1965	R. Singh	Palaeolithic Industries of Northern Bundelkhand.
24.	1966	Nisar Ahmed	Stone Age Cultures of the Upper Sona Valley.
25.	1966	R. S. Pappu	Pleistocene Studies in the Upper Krishna Basin.
26.	1966	M. S. Nagaraja Rao	Chalcolithic Cultures of the Deccan With Special Reference to North Karanataka.
27.	1966	S. N. Rao	Stone Age Cultures of Nalgonda District (A. P.).
28.	1966	M. L. K. Murthy	Stone Age Cultures of Chitoor District (A. P.).
29.	1966	Miss Malati Nagar	Ahar Culture—An Archaeological and Ethnographic Study.
30.	1968	B. G. Supekar	Pleistocene Stratigraphy and Prehistoric Archaeology of the Central Narmada Basin.
31.	1968	K. Paddayya	Pre and Proto-Historic Investigation of the Shorapur Doab.
32.	1968	K. Thimma Reddy	Prehistoric Cultures of the Cuddapah District (A. P.).
33.	1968	S. N. Tipnis	Contribution of Upasani Baba to Cultural Life of Maharashtra and India.
34.	1969	P. B. Gadre	Cultural Archaeology of Ahmadnagar during Nizam Shahi Period.
35.	1969	Mrs. Omi Manchanda	Study of the Harappan Pottery in Comparison with Pre-Harappan and Post-Harappan Proto-Historic

			Ceramic industries.
36.	1969	S. Sundra	Megaliths in North Karnataka.
37.	1969	R. D. Choudhary	Archaeology of the Brahmaputra Valley of Assam (Pre-ahom period)
38.	1970	Rehman Ali	Art and Architecture of the Kala-curies of Tripuri.
39.	1972	V. S. Lele	Late Quaternary Studies on the Bhadar Valley Surashtra.
40.	1973	Miss Suman Pandya	An Ethno-Archaeological Study of the Harappan and Post Harappan Cultures of Saurashtra.
41.	1973	Miss S. Guzdar	Quaternary Environment and Stone Age Cultures of the Konkan Cosstal, Maharashtra.